I Love You... STILL

To Wanda —
Thanks for
sharing your words
of wisdom! Your friend —
Martha
Bolton

Martha Bolton

I Love You... STILL

To Keep the Love, Ya Gotta Laugh

Fleming H. Revell

A Division of Baker Book House Co
Grand Rapids, Michigan 49516

Published by Fleming H. Revell
a division of Baker Book House Company
P.O. Box 6287, Grand Rapids, MI 49516-6287

Printed in the United States of America

Library of Congress Cataloging-in-Publication Data

Bolton, Martha, 1951–
    I love you . . . still : to keep the love, you gotta laugh /
Martha Bolton.
      p.   cm.
   ISBN 0-8007-1774-0
    1. Spouses—Religious life. 2. Marriage—Religious
aspects—Christianity. 3. Spouses—Religious life—Humor.
4. Marriage—Religious aspects—Christianity—Humor.
I. Title.
BV4596.M3 M65   2000
248.8'44—dc21   00-029118

Unless otherwise indicated Scripture quotations are taken from the King
James Version of the Bible.

For current information about all releases from Baker Book House, visit our
web site:
                     http://www.bakerbooks.com

Contents

Foreword

THIS IS BOB-I'VE-BEEN-MARRIED-FOR-SIXTY-SIX-YEARS-HOPE.

Recently, I boasted about being married for sixty-six years and was asked: "What is the secret to your long marriage?"

"Dolores," I said.

That's true—a little simplified, perhaps—but true. Of course, sharing common interests doesn't hurt. We both have a passion for golf, we both love dogs, and we're both avid San Diego Charger fans. But, most of all, from the very beginning of our marriage, we've shared laughter.

There are always a few surprises in married life—you know, those things that were not writ-

11

ten into the script. All of us have to ad-lib our way through some turbulence, trials, touch-and-go situations. And a sense of humor helps us do that. If you can laugh together, you can get through anything.

Hey, wait a minute! Why am I doing "schtick" about marriage when you're holding in your hands a wonderfully entertaining book about the subject? It's by Martha Bolton, who is a pretty solid writer. I know. She wrote jokes for me for more years than she wants to admit.

Martha knows all about being married. That wasn't in her contract, however. She and her husband, Russ, managed that entirely on their own. On their fifteenth anniversary, her colleagues presented her with a cue card with one of her jokes about marriage written on it. We all signed it. I wrote "Try to catch up with us."

Marriage, laughter, and joy—that's what this book is all about. Have an enjoyable time with it. I did.

Acknowledgments

To my parents and my uncles and aunts, who showed me by example what marriage commitment truly means.

To my husband and children for their love and patience, but most of all, for their sense of family.

To Linda Holland, my editor and "sugar-free" buddy. *Found any good chocolates lately?*

And to lovers everywhere who have learned that the happiest married couples aren't those who have never seen trouble, but those who have kept their focus on the flowers while laughing at the thorns.

1
I've Grown Accustomed to Your Clutter

Be ye kind one to another, tenderhearted, forgiving one another, even as God for Christ's sake hath forgiven you.

Ephesians 4:32

THEY say opposites attract. It must be true because when it comes to clutter, my husband and I are like night and day. I'm one of those people who has a hard time throwing things away. My husband is the exact opposite. He throws *everything* away—broken appliances (a toaster causes *one* lousy kitchen fire and it's history), junk mail (in the very week it arrives), and old phone books (for some reason, he thinks the ones listing party lines are outdated). As you can see, the man has a major problem.

I keep *everything*—coupons that expired during the cold war, every paper my sons ever doodled on, and the voter's pamphlet from the '88 election.

Nowhere is this difference between us more evident than in the bedroom. On my husband's nightstand are his Bible, pictures of the family, and some little ceramic houses that remind him of Skid Row, where he worked as a police sergeant.

My side of the bed looks like Skid Row. There are papers, books, magazines, miscellaneous snacks in varying degrees of decomposition, and the files to whatever projects I happen to be working on. There's so much clutter there, if I ever rolled off the bed, my family wouldn't find me for a week. The upside to all my clutter is I never have to call in an exterminator. The ants just die of suffocation.

Because my husband doesn't understand this way of living, the subject of clutter comes up often. I listen to his concerns, of course, but still it amazes me that the same man who can't bear the fact that I'm hanging onto a four-year-old Sears catalog will wear the same T-shirt until there are so many holes in it, it looks like a doily. But I digress.

To keep peace, we've both made some new vows. I've promised to throw away at least twenty pieces of paper each day, and he's promised to quit dusting the light bulbs. It's a workable compromise. And, to tell you the truth, it really is freeing to toss out some of the clutter I've been holding onto all these years—not the important, irreplaceable things, but the junk, those "had to have it" souvenirs that I don't really have to have anymore.

We need to be just as diligent at tossing out those things that clutter up our relationships, too—old hurts, unfinished arguments, unforgiveness. They only take up room in our minds and drain us of the energy needed for what's really important in life.

Clutter—wherever it is, we should be doing our best to get rid of it. If you ask me, though, my husband should be thanking me for my piles of clutter around the house. If it wasn't for all that climbing he has to do to get over it, who knows what shape his heart would be in!

A Date to Communicate

Are you allowing something to clutter your relationship with each other?

Him:

Her:

List the advantages to clearing out the above clutter from your lives:

Him:

Her:

> By all means marry; if you get a good wife, you'll become happy; if you get a bad one, you'll become a philosopher.
>
> Socrates

2
Comfort Zone

And let us consider one another to provoke unto love and to good works.

Hebrews 10:24

ONE of the funniest sketches I ever saw featured an older actor playing a man who was on a date with a girl about half his age. In an attempt to convince her that he was still young and dashing, he had used black shoe polish to cover his graying hair. It worked great until the restaurant where they were eating began to get a little warm, and narrow streams of black sweat started making their way down his forehead. Oblivious to what was happening, he continued flirting, wiping his brow every so often and smearing the black goo all over his face.

While I wouldn't recommend combing shoe polish in your hair to keep the excitement in your marriage, it is important to work at looking your best for your mate.

Have you let yourself go over the years? Is your idea of dressing up tying the belt on your bathrobe? Have you had curlers in your hair for so long your television reception now depends on it? Will you only lift a barbell when it's blocking the freezer door and keeping you from the Breyer's? Do you even bother ironing your muumuu anymore?

Don't get me wrong. Being comfortable with your spouse is a good thing. Being able to be yourself, to be real, to relax and let go of the pretenses is healthy. The problem is, though, along with those pretenses, some of us have let ourselves go, too.

Why do we do it? Good question.

We don't think anything of dressing up for our co-workers, our church friends, our ladies' or men's group. We'll spend the money to get our hair done for job interviews and out-of-town company. We even buy new clothes for the strangers we're going to meet on vacation. But when it comes to the one person we spend most of our time with, it's the coffee-stained jogging suit and earless bunny slippers.

Remember how it used to be when you were dating, how much you both focused on appearance? Your sweetheart was the one you were trying to impress then. You'd try on outfit after outfit searching for that perfect look. You'd stand in front of the mirror for twenty minutes styling and restyling your hair. How you looked to him or her was important to you. It still should be.

So, go ahead, wipe off that deep-heating ointment and replace it with a little cologne. Try out a new hairstyle and start toning up those muscles. Put on that outfit you've been saving. You're special to your spouse. Treat yourself like it.

A Date to Communicate

If you could have a "night out on the town" with just your spouse, where would you go and what would you do?

Him:

Her:

Sometimes change is good, but the one quality of my spouse that I hope he/she never changes is:

His answer:

Her answer:

> The reason why couples fall in love (stay together or break up) is because of how they feel about themselves when they are around the other person. Liking YOURSELF when you're around the other person can be one of the biggest pluses in your marriage.
>
> Al Fike
> Comedian

3
What a View!

Blessed be the Lord, who daily loadeth us
with benefits.

Psalm 68:19

RECENTLY, my husband and I moved from
California to Nashville, Tennessee. We drove
Interstate 40, and on the way we saw some in-
credible scenery. There weren't any signs advis-
ing travelers to stop and take a look at the view.
There didn't need to be any. You couldn't miss it.

Farther down the road, when I finally did see a
sign with the words "Scenic View" printed on it, the
scene didn't look that much different than what we

had been driving through for the past sixty miles. Still, travelers pulled over, got out of their cars, cameras in hand, and excitedly started snapping away.

I wanted to stop and ask everyone, "What's the matter with you people? Haven't you been paying attention?" I couldn't believe they actually needed a sign to point out the beauty that had been right in front of them all along just because someone finally told them to "look."

Unfortunately, that's how some of us are in our relationships. We look at our loved ones day in and day out. We speed right past them either physically, emotionally, or both, taking everything they do, say, and are for granted. Just like those tourists, we fail to see the beauty that's staring us in the face.

Too bad there aren't posted signs along life's journey telling us when we're about to miss out on something spectacular. But life doesn't come with "Scenic View" signs. It's up to us to slow down and look.

A Date to Communicate

Write a love letter to your spouse. List the things you appreciate most.

What I appreciate most about my wife is:

What I appreciate most about my husband is:

I keep him from being boring and he keeps me out of jail!

Nan and Dennis Allen
Writers, musician, composer
Married twenty-four years

4

Fashionably Late

The LORD preserveth the faithful.

Psalm 31:23

MY husband is very nostalgic, especially when it comes to his wardrobe. He watches the History Channel to get fashion tips and will wear the same dress shirt until it's bid on by the Smithsonian. Once in a while, though, he lets down his guard and gives in to his wilder side—like the day he finally decided to buy a leisure suit.

It was several decades ago, but I'll never forget it. I had been trying to convince him to get one ever since they first appeared on the fashion scene, but he always had an excuse. "They're too flashy." "Their lapels are too big." "They're just not *me.*"

Then one day, out of the clear blue he announced he wanted to go shopping for a leisure suit. I don't know what made him change his mind, but I wasn't about to let the moment pass.

I grabbed the car keys and drove him as quickly as I could to a local department store. We walked straight to Men's Wear and easily located the sweater racks, the shirt racks, and the jeans racks, but leisure suits were nowhere in sight.

"They're probably upstairs," my husband said as we took off toward the escalator. But the leisure suits weren't upstairs either. They weren't upstairs, they weren't downstairs, they weren't *anywhere.*

Bewildered, my husband tracked down a salesclerk and asked, "Excuse me, sir, but do you know where I would find your leisure suits?"

The clerk looked up at my husband only briefly, then said smugly, "Sure. Back in the 70s."

Fashions come and go. What's hot and trendy today is embarrassingly out of style tomorrow. But marriage isn't a trend. You don't wear a wedding ring because it goes with your new outfit. You wear it because it symbolizes a commitment, a promise, a bond between two people. A bond that was meant to outlast all the trends—the bell bottoms, mini skirts, maxi skirts, Hawaiian shirts, and, yes, even leisure suits.

Marriage—it's one of the few things in life that never goes out of style.

A Date to Communicate

Why do you think marriage is more than a trend?

His answer:

Her answer:

In what ways can you ensure that your marriage never goes "out of style"?

His answer:

Her answer:

George proposed to me on the first date and I knew he was the man for me the moment I checked out his closet. Every article of clothing he ever owned was stuffed in that closet. I figured a grown man who still held onto his kindergarten paint smock wasn't afraid of commitment. You know what? I was right.

As for how we've lasted so long, what can I say? We broke every rule in the book and went to bed mad on more occasions than we can count. We've survived three kids, four grandkids, umpteen houses, one failed business; numerous cars, dogs, cats, hamsters, and two earthquakes. Yet, as far as I can tell, the old paint smock is still holding up. Isn't love grand?

Margaret Brownley
Romance novelist, author
of twenty books
Married thirty-seven years

5
One Man's Encouragement

I will instruct thee and teach thee in the way which thou shalt go: I will guide thee with mine eye.

Psalm 32:8

ACCORDING to my husband, I'm bilingual. I'm fluent in both English and Nag. But what he calls nagging, I prefer to call *compulsive encouragement*. No matter how hard I try to keep my nagging—I mean, compulsive encouragement—to myself, I can't help but share it. I encourage him to mow the lawn, take out the trash, pick up his socks, paint the house, eat slower, drive more carefully—the encouragement goes on and on and on.

But this is nothing new. Throughout history, wives have been known for their penchant for compulsive encouragement. When Noah was loading the ark, do you think for a minute that his wife didn't encourage Noah to remember to pack the air freshener? And every time Napoleon posed for a picture, I'm sure Josephine had words of encouragement for him, too. "Just this once, Napoleon, can't you take your hand out of your pocket and pose like all the other men?"

All this encouragement started with Eve, you know. The Bible may not go into a lot of detail when it says that Eve gave the apple to Adam and he ate it, but I'm sure if we were to get our hands on the videotape and play it back, the scene probably went something like this:

"Adam! You gonna sleep all day?! Get out of that bed and come eat this apple! I've been telling you for years that you need to eat more roughage, but do you ever listen to me? No! Why do I even bother?"

Adam did eat the fruit, and afterwards I'm sure he had some compulsive encouragement for Eve, too. Again, without the videotape it's hard to know how the conversation went verbatim, but it was probably like this: "C'mon, Eve. God's waiting for us! He's not very happy and you're making us late. How long does it take to put on three leaves?"

Nagging or encouragement, whatever you call it, has been around since the beginning of time. And you have to admit, sometimes a little nagging is good for us. Who knows? If Moses had listened to his wife and asked directions, maybe they would have reached the promised land in twenty years instead of forty. Again, there's no videotape, but it does make you wonder, doesn't it?

A Date to Communicate

If you're a compulsive encourager, what do you feel is the true emotion behind it? Control? Fear? Perfectionist tendencies? Something else?

Him:

Her:

Why do you think it's important to sometimes keep our opinions to ourselves?

Him:

Her:

> I'd go to the end of the world for my husband. Of course, if he'd just stop and ask directions, I wouldn't have to.
>
> Martha Bolton

> Always make time for your wife and family.
>
> John Mathias
> Director, Lillenas Music and Drama Publishing Company

6
Shop 'Til Who Drops?

Charity suffereth long, and is kind.
1 Corinthians 13:4

IF I've learned anything from marriage, it's this: when it comes to shopping, there are distinct differences between a man and a woman. For instance:

The first thing a woman looks for is a sale.
The first thing a man looks for is a chair.
A woman's idea of comparison shopping is comparing every item in every mall within a hundred-mile radius of her house.

A man's idea of comparison shopping is comparing a new shirt with his old shirt and opting to stick with the old one.

There is no limit to the amount of packages a woman will carry.

The same man who can easily benchpress 150 pounds will complain of heart palpitations and buckling knees under the weight of a package of tube socks.

A woman will gladly make six trips to the dressing room to try on clothes.

A man gets exhausted just trying on clothes in his mind.

A woman will sample every bottle of perfume on the counter.

A man is happy with a cologne called "Generic."

A woman looks for the smallest size she could possibly fit into.

A man isn't aware that clothing comes in sizes.

The ideal shopping situation for a woman is a moonlight madness sale.

The ideal shopping situation for a man is a football game playing on all the television sets in the electronics department.

A woman considers shopping therapy.

After shopping, a man considers therapy.

To further illustrate the difference between male and female shoppers, the following dialogue is provided:

	Wife	Husband
1st store	"Thanks for coming shopping with me, honey."	"My feet hurt."
2nd store	"How does this dress look on me?"	"My feet hurt."
3rd store	"Maybe I'll find a better buy here."	"My feet hurt."
4th store	"What I really need is a pair of slacks."	"My feet hurt."
5th store	"Speaking of feet, aren't these shoes cute?"	"My feet hurt."
6th store	"I'm glad I waited. They're cheaper here."	"My feet hurt."
7th store	"I haven't found a thing all night. I guess we'll just cut through that sporting goods store and go on home."	"Sporting goods store?"
8th store	"My feet hurt."	"Well, I *could* use a new golf club."

A Date to Communicate

What is it about shopping that you hate or love most?

His answer:

Her answer:

What kind of compromise could you both reach to make shopping a more pleasurable experience?

His answer:

Her answer:

> Enjoy what you can and endure what you must.
>
> Goethe

7
Listen Up!

Now I beseech you, brethren, by the name of our Lord Jesus Christ, that ye all speak the same thing, and that there be no divisions among you.

1 Corinthians 1:10

ONE night not long ago I got a good education in communication. Some out-of-town friends had called my husband to see if we could get together for dinner the following evening. He explained that he had a meeting scheduled that would probably last until around six o'clock, but said we could meet after that. It was agreed that the women would arrange the time and place.

The next afternoon the man's wife called and we decided to meet at 6:30 at a restaurant about twenty miles north of our house. I phoned my husband at the police station where he worked to tell him of the arrangements, but he had already left for his meeting. I left a message detailing all the necessary information: the restaurant where he would be meeting us, the time, and the beeper number of our friends should he need to communicate with them. Satisfied that everything was going smoothly, I went ahead and left for the restaurant.

My husband's meeting lasted longer than he expected. When it finally adjourned, he was handed my phone message, read it, then paged our friends to tell them that he didn't think he was going to be able to make it. He assumed I was already with them and his absence wouldn't affect the dinner plans. They assumed I was with him, and since neither of us was going to be able to make it, they went home.

Meanwhile, I assumed everyone was en route to the previously arranged restaurant, where I sat patiently waiting at a table for six. I couldn't help but feel a little conspicuous as the restaurant was crowded and they obviously needed the space. Every time our waitress asked if the rest of my party was coming, I assured her they were. I even ordered two appetizer trays just to prove my confidence.

To add insult to injury, the people at the table next to me were celebrating a birthday. As a line of waiters walked in my direction with a lit candle on a slice of cake, singing their own arrangement of the Happy Birthday chorus, I could sense every eye in the restaurant looking pitifully in my direction. The "birthday table" was just out of view of the rest of the customers, so it appeared as though I was sitting at an empty table for six celebrating my birthday alone. Needless to say, it was a long night.

It's easy to miscommunicate, to get our wires crossed. Luckily, this miscommunication was easy to clear up and only resulted in a few wasted hours and a little embarrassment. Other miscommunications can take a little longer to clear up. But it's imperative to clear them up because, left unresolved, they could eventually destroy a marriage.

A Date to Communicate

Is there a miscommunication that you need to clear up in your relationship?

Him:

Her:

Why do you think it's important to listen, *really listen,* to what your spouse is saying?

Him:

Her:

> Communication is the founda-
> tion for a successful marriage.
> Listen to what your partner says,
> not just what you want to hear.
>   Carol Doering
>   Writer

8

Is That What I Said?

Wives, submit yourselves unto your own husbands, as it is fit in the Lord. Husbands, love your wives, and be not bitter against them.

Colossians 3:18–19

IF you're married, you've said them. If you're engaged, you're about to say them. What are they? The marriage vows. But do couples today realize what those vows *really* mean? Considering the current divorce rate, many of them don't. So to clear up any misconceptions, the following revised marriage ceremony is provided.

I, (insert name), take thee, (insert name) to be my lawfully wedded (husband/wife). To have and to hold from this day forward.

For better or worse, which includes:

—when her "honey do" list is longer than the Congressional Record

—when he wakes you up at 4:00 A.M. making those strange noises with his adenoids

—when her parents announce they'll be staying two weeks longer than expected

For richer, for poorer, which includes:

—when she can't recall whether check #496 was written to the paperboy or the mortgage company

—when he forgets and leaves the sprinklers running during a three-day getaway

—when the monthly telephone bill arrives in hardback

In sickness and in health, including but not limited to:

—when you burn your hand on the curling iron she left plugged in on the sink

—when you're doubled over with stomach cramps from that liver and dumplings recipe she got off one of those cooking shows

—when she really *does* have a headache

Forsaking all others, in other words:

—you promise to turn off your favorite soap while he's trying to tell you about his day

—you promise to turn off that football game while she's trying to tell you about her day

As long as we both shall live.

Perhaps if we all did more of the above, this last one might not be so hard to live up to.

A Date to Communicate

Would you say that you've been honoring your marriage vows to the best of your ability?

Him:

Her:

In what ways do you think you can improve?

Him:

Her:

Overheard at an anniversary celebration:

> Thirty-five years ago we said, "I do," and that's the last thing we've agreed on in thirty-five years!

> The secret to our marriage is to always communicate with an open mind and a gentle heart.

Matt Bolton
Musician, telecommunications

Nicole Bolton
Student, homemaker

9
Fault Lines

Confess your faults one to another, and
pray one for another, that ye may be healed.

James 5:16

THERE are two ways to apologize. First, there's
the straightforward "I did it and I'm sorry" kind
of apology. Then, there's the one that goes something like this:

"So, are you going to apologize?"
"I did already."
"Saying 'What's for dinner?' is not an apology."

"You know what I meant."

"You need to say it."

"Okay, maybe I, it's possible that, well, perhaps I was, well, you know . . ."

"Wrong? You were wrong. Why can't you just admit it?"

"I just did."

"No, you didn't."

"I did too. Now can we move on to something else?"

"As soon as you admit you were wrong."

"If you missed it the first time, I'm not going to say it again."

"You never said it the first time."

"Never said what?"

"I'm sorry."

"Apology accepted."

It doesn't matter how infallible we think we are, the fact of the matter is we're imperfect. We're going to mess up from time to time. That's a given. Since the beginning of time, only one perfect person has ever walked this earth, and He never married. Admitting our mistakes and being able to say we're sorry doesn't make us the lesser partner in a relationship. It makes us human. It also makes us more lovable, both to ourselves and to our partner.

A Date to Communicate

Do you feel you're quick to apologize when you're wrong?

Him:

Her:

Why do you think it's hard for people to apologize when they're wrong?

Him:

Her:

> He understands badly who listens badly.
>
> Welsh proverb

10
In Other Words

A wholesome tongue is a tree of life.

Proverbs 15:4

Do you know that what you hear your spouse say isn't always what she or he is saying? For instance:

If you hear . . .
"Honey, I wish you wouldn't spend so much time at the golf course."

What she's saying is . . .
"I sold your clubs at the garage sale."

If you hear . . .
"How about going out to eat tonight, sweetie?"

What she's saying is . . .
"It'll take a few hours for the smoke to clear out of the kitchen anyway."

If you hear . . .
"How much longer are you going to be in that bathroom?"

What he's saying is . . .
"Will that one-year light bulb be enough?"

If you hear . . .
"Honey, can you help me for a minute?"

What she's saying is . . .
"Honey, since there are only two minutes left in the basketball game and both teams are tied, wouldn't this be a great time to rearrange the furniture?"

If you hear . . .
"I'll be ready in just another minute, sweetheart."

What she's saying is . . .
"Get ready to watch your fingernails grow."

If you hear . . .
"Do I still look as pretty to you as the day we got married?"

What she's saying is . . .
"Do you want to sleep on the bed or the sofa tonight?"

If you hear . . .
"I'm looking forward to your mother coming to spend a week with us."

What he's saying is . . .
"I think I'll schedule that root canal now. The pain will seem minimal by comparison."

If you hear . . .
"I don't have a thing to wear."

What's she's saying is . . .
"You wouldn't believe the cute outfit I saw today at Macy's."

If you hear . . .
"I thought about you all day today."

What she's saying is . . .
"They preempted my soap this week."

51

If you hear . . .
"I can fix this myself."

What he's saying is . . .
"Give me six hours to take it all apart, misplace four of the screws, make it completely unrepairable, *then* I'll call a repairman."

If you hear . . .
"Sweetheart, you've got my undivided attention tonight."

What he's saying is . . .
"There's no football on TV tonight."

If you hear . . .
"Tell me again how much you love me."

What she's saying is . . .
"You'll find what's left of the car in the driveway."

A Date to Communicate

Do you feel like there's been a breakdown in your communication lately?

Him:

Her:

Can you think of a time when a miscommunication made a small problem a big problem?

Him:

Her:

> After over twenty years of marriage I have decided that the key ingredient to a successful marriage is not really a secret—it's God. My wife and I always do our best to follow the many examples that the Lord has provided in the Bible. We make our lives evolve around each other, in fact, I try to take my wife's needs and wants into consideration in every decision that I make. My whole life is

my wife and family. The Lord has shown me that I must provide and take care of them until as the famous marriage vow states ". . . death do us part." We need to make sure that we know and understand exactly what these words mean. It is also very important to know and understand what "unconditional love" really means and apply it to our marriage!

Frank Bush
Building inspector,
City of Los Angeles

11

The Opposition

Have peace one with another.

Mark 9:50

My husband is a twenty-eight-year veteran of the Los Angeles Police Department. I'm a comedy writer. I'm not sure which one of us sees more comedy and which one of us faces more danger, but we do see life from two totally opposing viewpoints. He's guarded with most people. I'm naively trusting. We both get surprised sometimes.

One of my favorite Bob Hope stories perfectly illustrates how our careers have had to co-exist.

One day when California was hit by an early morning earthquake, both my husband and I received calls to go to work. His call was from the police department to help with the disaster. My call came from Bob Hope, who asked me to start writing jokes about the temblor. My call got through first.

To say the least, life's been interesting having these two occupations under one roof. But after more than a quarter-century of marriage, we can attest to the fact that even opposites can live happily ever after. Although it requires extra patience at times and a healthy helping of understanding, it can work. You both just have to want it to.

A Date to Communicate

In what ways do you think you and your spouse are opposites?

Him:

Her:

In what ways do you think you're similar?

Him:

Her:

> The small, intimate gestures mean the most. My husband warms my side of the bed on cold winter nights before I climb in. He makes meat loaf in a heart shape. How can I resist?
>
> Mary Scott
> Poet, newspaper columnist
> Married four years

12
Be Our Guest

Walk in love, as Christ also hath loved us, and hath given himself for us an offering and a sacrifice to God for a sweetsmelling savour.

Ephesians 5:2

As newlyweds, neither my husband nor I knew very much about entertaining. I didn't realize how little he knew, though, until one night when we invited another couple over for dinner.

After dining on an exquisite meal (one of Stouffer's more expensive entrees), we moved into the living room for some coffee and conversation. The conversation lasted a lot longer than the coffee, but I was enjoying it. My husband was, too, until he remembered he had to go to work the next day.

Not wanting to waste any time dropping subtle hints that they might not pick up on, he merely stood up and announced, "We're going to bed now. You can let yourselves out."

Thankfully, he's become more socially aware over the years. We both have. Sometimes, though, while remembering to be hospitable to others, we forget to be hospitable to those closest to us. If he asks for a glass of water, she reminds him where the sink is. If she asks for help with the dishes, he suddenly doesn't understand English. It's as if we're keeping a running tally and know precisely when we're being asked to do or give more than our agreed-upon 50 percent.

But hospitality isn't something reserved just for company. We should readily offer it to each other, too.

A Date to Communicate

In what ways can you show more hospitality to your spouse?

Him:

Her:

In what ways would you like your spouse to show more hospitality to you?

His answer:

Her answer:

> My secret to a successful marriage begins with trust. I trust my husband Frank more than any other person. Whatever my failures (I have had one or two) I can count on him to keep them to himself and not confide in others. We also enjoy spending time together and with our kids at home, school, church, sports, etc. Frank never forgets special occasions and often

surprises me with little gifts for no apparent reason other than he loves me. We have our difficult moments, but God is our strength and we can always share everything with Him.

Judy Bush
Wife, mother, nurse, maid, cook, gardener, taxi driver, accountant, etc. for building inspector and his offspring

13
None of Our Business

My little children, let us not love in word,
neither in tongue; but in deed and in truth.

1 John 3:18

MAYBE it's just me, but there seems to be a difference between how men and women set up a business. According to my husband, the first step in any new business endeavor is ordering business cards. As soon as he gets an idea for a business, he starts designing his cards. He has a different business card for every business he's ever started or even thought of starting. He has thousands of them, most of which are being used as scratch paper now. Business cards are cheaper when you order them in bulk, he says.

Not only will my husband order business cards every time a new business idea crosses his mind, but he'll also make lists of everything he'll need for his new home office. The list usually includes a new fax, a new computer, the very latest in computer software, a new desk and chair, business stationery, a separate telephone line, a printer, a paper shredder, and well, he basically just goes through the Office Depot catalog and circles every item.

I, on the other hand, have always believed one should make money first and buy fancy equipment later. That's why I haven't updated my office in years. My computer has about as much memory as a politician after an election, and the thirteen-year-old fax I'm still using saves me money because it doubles as a paper shredder, too. It eats every important document I feed it. And business cards? I've been a writer for over twenty years and I still don't have current business cards. But I get by. I simply hand new clients one of my bank deposit slips. It has all the pertinent information on it and, who knows, maybe someone will accidentally deposit some money into my account someday.

Obviously, the best way to run a new business is somewhere in the middle. You need to invest some money, but you don't have to go overboard with your expenditures.

It's the same with a marriage. Showing our spouses we love them shouldn't drain us financially. If we can't afford that new diamond watch, we may have to go with something a little less pricey—like maybe flowers, a nice dinner out, or just writing a love letter on some nice stationery. The point is to pay tribute to the one we love, not interest to MasterCard and Visa. If we spend too much on a single expression of love, we may have to go for months, perhaps even years, before we can express our love again. But by expressing our love using the resources we have, there'll be no limit on how often we can do it. And what husband or wife can resist *that?*

A Date to Communicate

What is the most thoughtful thing your spouse has ever done for you?

Him:

Her:

This week, plan to do something thoughtful for your spouse.

Him:

Her:

Marriage is the most predictable "cause and effect" bank account that exists in the universe! Mutually make deposits of love, understanding, trust, emotional support, or unselfish giving and you watch the account grow daily in an abundance of dividends. A wealth of love, trust, emotional support, and care multiplies and compounds. But make deposits of mistrust, conditional love, greed, or unilateral selfishness and there are no dividends to be enjoyed, only bankruptcy.

Tom Bruner
Composer, arranger,
and conductor of music

14
A Very Cold Shoulder

Let nothing be done through strife or vainglory; but in lowliness of mind let each esteem other better than themselves.

Philippians 2:3

A priest and a nun got lost in a severe snow-storm one night, and after driving for what seemed like forever, they eventually saw a small cabin off in the distance. Exhausted and cold, they tried the door. It was unlocked, so they decided to go in and try to get some sleep. Perhaps by morning the storm would be over and they could find their way back to the main highway.

Inside, there were blankets, a sleeping bag, and one bed. The priest said, "Sister, you take the bed and the blankets. I'll sleep on the floor in the sleeping bag."

The priest crawled into the bag, zipped it up, and was just beginning to fall asleep when the nun said, "Father, I'm cold." Being the thoughtful and caring man that he was, the priest unzipped the sleeping bag, got up, and got the sister a blanket.

He then returned to his sleeping bag and zipped it up. He had barely drifted off to sleep again when the nun said, "Father, I'm still very cold."

The priest gave a slight sigh which only he could hear, unzipped the bag, and got her another blanket. This time he didn't even get his eyes closed when once again she said, "Father, I'm soooo cold."

Exasperated, he laid there for a moment, then finally broke the uncomfortable silence. "Sister," he said, "I have an idea. We're out here all by ourselves, miles and miles from the nearest town. No one will ever know what happened. Why don't we just pretend we're married."

The nun thought for a moment and then said, "Sounds good to me."

So the priest said, "Get up and get your own stupid blanket!"

Source unknown

This joke is funny because there's a degree of truth in it. Too often when the honeymoon is over, our manners slip out the door with it. We go from saying "I do" to whining "Do I have to?" When she asks for that blanket, he pretends to be asleep. If he asks for the remote control, she kicks it to him while grumbling something about his ability to get up and get it himself. A good number of us have forgotten what it means to cherish that one we promised to cherish forever. We've forgotten what it means to serve.

Jesus demonstrated this principle so often that maybe He meant for us to get the point. We're supposed to put others' needs before our own. We're supposed to give before we think about getting.

Marriage isn't meeting each other halfway. It's each one going above and beyond what is expected of them. It's giving 100 percent of yourself to the other person. It's going that extra mile without ever checking the mileage.

A Date to Communicate

In what ways do you feel you're going that extra mile for your spouse?

Him:

Her:

In what ways do you feel your spouse is going that extra mile for you?

Him:

Her:

> When we came into the house, we kissed. When one of us left the house, we kissed. And we always held hands. If the one you're thinking about marrying isn't your best friend, pass.
>
> Carole Shaw
> Founder, *Big Beautiful Woman* magazine
> Married forty years

15
Get Away

> Better is a handful with quietness, than both the hands full with travail and vexation of spirit.
>
> Ecclesiastes 4:6

COUNTLESS couples on the brink of separation have saved their marriages by attending marriage seminars or retreats. Even more couples have gone simply to give their marriage a tune up, a refresher course.

Getting away from the kids, the phone, the in-laws, and the bills, and focusing solely on your partner can give your marriage a brand-new perspective. But how do you know when it's time for you and your spouse to go on a marriage retreat? The following checklist might help:

You Know It's Time for a Marriage Retreat When:

She sets the table and you're the only one who gets a paper plate.

Lately, the family dog has been getting better cuts of meat than you.

All week long she's only been making her side of the bed.

Life is so stressful at your house, you've been in the bathtub since August.

Your picture in his wallet has been replaced by an Albertsons' discount card.

The last night out he planned involved the laundromat.

The only time he reaches for your hand is when you're reaching for your credit cards.

With all your fighting, more flying objects can be seen in your house than at Roswell.

You catch yourself trying to figure out a way to drop the kids off at church for summer Vacation Bible School and pick them up after the Christmas pageant.

The last picnic lunch you shared was some crackers and Cheeze Whiz you found under the front seat when the car broke down.

Her idea of spending a nice quiet evening alone involves you going somewhere.

Now when you give her flowers, they're seeds in a packet and they come with a shovel.

But you really know it's time to go on a marriage retreat when you start getting Pearl Harbor Day and your anniversary mixed up.

In actuality, any time is a good time for a marriage retreat. It's healthy to get away for a weekend to learn more about love, marriage, and each other. And if you can't afford the expense of a retreat, just get away alone for an afternoon drive, a picnic, or a walk in the park. You're a couple. Sometimes you have to close out the rest of the world and remind yourselves of that.

A Date to Communicate

Do you feel you spend enough quiet time together?

Him:

Her:

Keeping within your budget, what can you do today to start planning a getaway?

Him:

Her:

Happy wife. Happy life.

Jeff Allen
Comedian
Married fifteen years

16

Uninvited Guests

Purge out therefore the old leaven, that
ye may be a new lump, as ye are unleavened.

1 Corinthians 5:7

A number of years ago, my husband met a
man who offered to give us a winter's worth of
free firewood. We lived in southern California at
the time, so we figured that'd be about one log.
It turned out to be an entire cord of old wood
from a dilapidated barn he was tearing down.
We didn't really need it, but because it was free
we figured it couldn't hurt.

We kept some of the wood in a basket next to our fireplace; the remainder we kept out on the patio. Even though that winter didn't bring any of those famous southern California blizzards, we did get to use some of the firewood. And apparently, we weren't the only ones.

A few weeks after bringing the firewood into our home, I began noticing little piles of sawdust building up on the floor next to the sofa. The arms of our sofa were made out of wood—wood that now seemed to be disintegrating before our very eyes.

When I pointed this out to my husband, he commented that it was probably just some sawdust left over from the last time I made meatloaf. He was partly right. It did turn out to be sawdust, but it wasn't the kind you'd find in the kitchen. It was the kind you'd find when you've got termites making an all-you-can-eat buffet out of your furniture.

Since we had recently purchased the house and it had passed a rigorous termite inspection, it didn't take us long to figure out where these uninvited guests were coming from.

The wood, of course. Upon closer examination, we discovered the wood was infested with termites! That "free" gift ended up costing us our sofa, an antique wooden shelf, and an expensive termite treatment. Too bad we hadn't paid more attention to what we were bringing into our home.

Likewise, we need to pay attention to what harmful things we're bringing into our marriage. On the surface, these things may seem like they're not costing us a thing. What possible harm could they do? In reality, though, they may be steadily eating away at our relationship, and we won't even realize the damage they're causing until all we have left is a pile of sawdust.

A Date to Communicate

Have you brought something or someone into your lives that might be eating away at your relationship?

Him:

Her:

Is it worth what you might be risking?

Him:

Her:

> There's no problem between
> the two of us that's bigger than
> the relationship and friendship.
>
> Kevin Wines
> Writer, comedian

17

In Sickness and in Health

Do all things without murmurings.

Philippians 2:14

TWENTY years ago my husband had a cyst removed from his hand. He can still recite the medical report verbatim. Men seem to remember their surgeries, sicknesses, toothaches, eye strain, and other physical ailments more than women. I'm talking in generalities, of course.

Most men don't react to sickness the way women do. If they get indigestion, the ambulance is in the driveway before you can unwrap the first Tums. If they smash their toe, they're the lead story on the 6 o'clock news asking for toenail donors. Maybe that's why God gave the job of birthing children to women. Even He can only take so much whimpering.

To better understand this male/female pain threshold, I've provided the following chart, appropriately titled . . .

Male/Female Pain Threshold

Pain felt by a woman and the equivalent pain felt by a man.

Women	Men
Pneumonia	Hay fever
Broken arm	Hit funny bone
Gall stone attack	Indigestion
Arthritis	Hangnail
Root canal	Plaque buildup
Cataract surgery	Eyelash in the eye
Appendicitis	One too many bowls of chili
Childbirth	Paper cut

A Date to Communicate

Was there ever a time when you were sick and didn't feel your spouse gave you enough attention?

Him:

Her:

What one thing would you like your spouse to do the next time you're sick?

Him:

Her:

> My advice for achieving a long and happy marriage is to find a loving partner willing to skate with you over thick and thin ice (mostly thin), and who shares your same values.
>
> George Brownley
> Film archivist, Paramount Studios
> Certified "Husband of the Year"

18
Thank You . . . I Think

Every good gift and every perfect gift is from above.

James 1:17

THE change is subtle. It happens gradually. You don't even notice it at first. Instead of getting a pretty dress or jewelry for your birthday, you get flannel pajamas. You tell him you like them, and you do to a certain extent. The feet will keep you warm in the winter, and those matching earmuffs are a nice touch, but down deep you know the gift represents a change in your relationship. Something's happened. He's seeing you differently. The romance has been replaced by practicality. Not that he doesn't love you, but a new dress isn't going to keep you warm at night. Flannel pajamas say love, too, only in a different way.

It happens to husbands, too, and the change is just as subtle. One year your wife is buying you "Wild Man" cologne, and the next year it's corn pads and a blood pressure monitor.

Don't get me wrong. Practicality certainly has its place in a marriage, but wouldn't it be nicer to open gifts or cards that remind us of those old feelings and rekindle that flame of romance? Corn pads just don't do that.

A Date to Communicate

Give three reasons why you made the right choice in choosing your spouse.

Him:

Her:

Write a note to your spouse and say something that you haven't said since the two of you were dating.

Him:

Her:

> A certain sort of talent is indispensable for people who would spend years together and not bore themselves to death.
>
> Robert Louis Stevenson

19
Last Words

Many waters cannot quench love, neither can the floods drown it.

Song of Solomon 8:7

I recently read about an eighty-nine-year-old man who had been married forty-four years to the same woman. He had made it a habit to tell his wife that he loved her before going to sleep each night. His thinking was simply this: in the tragic event something would happen to either one of them during their sleep, he wanted his last words to be "I love you."

It was a good habit.

After reading that article, I decided to make a list of some "last words" I've said to my husband just before drifting off to sleep. Had something happened to me during the night, these would be the words he would have had to remember me by:

"You're hogging all the blankets again!"

"Did you remember to pay the MasterCard bill?"

"Do you *really* have to eat that celery in bed?"

"That light's right in my eyes. If you have to read, can't you go into the other room?"

"You turned down the thermostat again, didn't you?"

"Were those your toenails, or is there a rake in the bed?"

"The toilet's still running. I thought you fixed that thing."

Maybe it's just me, but none of the above really seems memorable enough for a gravestone. I think that eighty-nine-year-old man had the right idea. "I love you" is probably the best parting phrase anyone could ever speak. Maybe we should all follow his lead.

A Date to Communicate

Why do you think it's important to end the day with an expression of your love?

Him:

Her:

What final words would you want your spouse to remember you by?

Him:

Her:

Marriage is much like a garden.
It requires attention in order to

enjoy its abundance. Neglected and unprotected for too long, it becomes overcome with infestation and devoured by predators. But with regular tending, it isn't an overwhelming chore and will yield a bountiful harvest. Anyone can have a garden, but a productive one is a thing of beauty. It reflects on its caretakers and is admired by all onlookers.

Lynn Edward Keesecker
Songwriter
Married fifteen years

20

Planting Time

With him is wisdom and strength, he hath counsel and understanding.

Job 12:13

MY friend, Diantha, gave my husband and me our very first dogwood tree. We planted it on April 17, our anniversary. That was a little over a week ago and so far it's still alive. Not a single blossom has fallen off. I point this out because, according to my husband, everything he plants dies. He's planted flowers that haven't made it, bushes and trees that have succumbed to the shock of the transplant, and vegetables that have gone on to that great salad bowl in the sky.

So why is this dogwood thriving? Because this time my husband asked the nursery attendant how to properly plant and care for the tree. He asked how deep to dig the hole, how much growth enhancer to use, and how to mix the mulch. This time he followed the advice of an expert.

Are you listening to expert advice, God's counsel, when it comes to your marriage? Are you giving your relationship the care it needs, making sure that it receives just the right amount of nutrition? Are you taking care of the weeds as soon as they start growing, or do you wait until they're so overgrown your marriage is gasping for air?

Much like a plant, marriage can't be ignored. It can't thrive without proper care. It needs to be protected from the frost of indifference, and nourished with love and understanding. If its needs are met, it'll grow tall and strong and fragrant. If its needs are ignored, it might not have a chance.

A Date to Communicate

Name three things that you can do to make sure your marriage grows properly.

Him:

Her:

This week, why not plant something that you can watch grow along with your love?

Him:

Her:

Have the same goals in mind.

Mosie and Wylene Lister
Songwriter
Southern Gospel Music Hall of Fame
Married fifty-three years

21

Full Circle

And the peace of God, which passeth all understanding, shall keep your hearts and minds through Christ Jesus.

Philippians 4:7

A marriage can go through a lot of changes over the years. It matures. Life happens. Struggles, heartaches, joys, and frustrations all serve to either solidify a marriage or tear it apart. Ideally, though, the longer a couple stays together, the more they come to understand each other, and the deeper their love grows.

To illustrate this point, the following nonscientific chart is provided:

Newlyweds	Ralphie?	Yes, snookums?
Five years married	Honey?	What is it, dear?
Ten years married	Ralph?	Yeah, hon'?
Twenty years married	Ralph Charles!	Whatever it is, I didn't do it.
Thirty years married	Ralph . . . Ralph . . . I'm talking to you, Ralph! Why don't you ever listen to me?	Did you say something, Agnes?
Forty years married	Ralph?!	Zzzzzzzz.
Fifty years married	Honey?	Yes, dear?
Sixty years married	Ralphie?	Yes, snookums?

A Date to Communicate

Do you feel your struggles and frustrations bring you closer together or farther apart?

93

Him:

Her:

How do you view struggles and frustrations? Do you consider them a part of life and go with the flow, or do you fight against the current and end up breaking apart?

Him:

Her:

> The secret to a happy marriage is prayer, patience, perseverance, and, if necessary, Prozac.
>
> Bill Gaither
> Songwriter
> Gospel Music Hall of Fame

22

Anonymous Gift

For ye yourselves are taught of God to love one another.

1 Thessalonians 4:9

A number of years ago, a good friend of mine confided that she was having some marital conflicts. Her complaint was that her husband hardly paid any attention to her, and as a result, her self-esteem was suffering and she was on the brink of leaving him.

Wanting to encourage her, I left an anonymous gift at her house one morning. The next time we talked, I asked how she and her husband were getting along. She was radiant. She explained how she'd found an anonymous gift one day that she knew had to be from him, and ever since then, their relationship had dramatically improved.

As far as I know, the husband didn't actually take credit for the gift. In fact, I don't think he even knew about it. Instead of telling her that I'd left the gift, I let her husband reap the benefits from it. That's all right. The gift did what I wanted it to do.

So often we think our marriages are beyond hope. We think that we (or our spouses) couldn't possibly say or do enough to repair the damage. But if a marriage can be destroyed by an accumulation of one hurt on top of another hurt on top of another hurt, it stands to reason that it can be healed by accumulation of acts of kindness, too.

A Date to Communicate

What was the last act of kindness that you showed to your spouse?

Him:

Her:

What is something that you could do today to show your spouse your love?

Him:

Her:

> One of the most important principles we try to live by in our marriage came straight from Dietrich Bonhoeffer. In a letter from prison to his niece, who was about to be married, he wrote something like, "You must forgive each other every day." (Of course,

that was paraphrased . . . he was much more eloquent than that.) We incorporated portions of Bonhoeffer's advice to his niece into our wedding ceremony, and that particular portion has stayed with us for sixteen years now.

Tim and Patty Freeman
Church drama consultants

23
Great Expectations

> And our hope of you is steadfast, knowing, that as ye are partakers of the sufferings, so shall ye be also of the consolation.
>
> 2 Corinthians 1:7

KEN and Barbie, Cinderella and Prince Charming, Mickey and Minnie Mouse—most of us grew up thinking our love, like theirs, was going to be perfect. In the fairy tale, Cinderella never nags Prince Charming. She doesn't tell him to take his feet off the royal coffee table, or make him get up early on Saturday morning to mow the castle grounds. And when's the last time you saw Ken greet Barbie in a torn and stained T-shirt that he's been wearing for the third day in a row? Ken doesn't belch after dinner or have car grease under his fingernails. His hair is always perfect, his body firm and tan, and he'll shop all day with Barbie as long as you prop him up against a wall or bend his legs over a chair. And what can be said about Mickey Mouse? He hasn't changed clothes in years and Minnie's never once said, "You're not going to wear *that* again, are you?"

Perfect marriages—unfortunately, there aren't any. In a real-life union, things don't run that smoothly. Mickey and Minnie don't have a mortgage to pay, Ken and Barbie have never gotten a call from the school that their daughter ditched again, and neither Cinderella nor Prince Charming has any control issues.

Fairy tales and pretend romances are good entertainment. They allow our imaginations to take us away to a land where everything, including marriage, is problem-free. But it's not reality. Marriage requires work. Sometimes a lot of work. But if you follow the right script, even real-life couples can live happily ever after.

A Date to Communicate

Do you feel your expectations of marriage have been unrealistic?

Him:

Her:

What are some achievable goals for your marriage?

Him:

Her:

> If you want peace in the house,
> do what your wife wants.
>
> African proverb

Let him have his way.

Sybil Ferren
Retired Penney's salesclerk
Married sixty-five years

24
Creating Moments

And let us consider one another to provoke unto love and to good works.

Hebrews 10:24

CONTRARY to what our florist, jeweler, travel agent, and even all those MasterCard promoters tell us, making memorable moments doesn't always require money or available credit. Often, all it takes is our time and a little bit of creativity.

While working on the "Bob Hope—The First 90 Years" television special, producer Don Mischner would often talk about creating "moments." He wanted the show to have plenty of them, and it did. War veterans shared memories with Bob; Dolores, Bob's wife of now over sixty-six years, sang a love song to him; and Presidents Ford, Carter, Reagan, Bush, and Clinton all wished the comedy legend a happy birthday. Even we writers had our fifteen minutes of fame (well, five anyway), exchanging stories on the nationally broadcast television special.

Moments. They're the secret to good entertainment. They can also be the secret to a good marriage.

If you're not already creating moments that you and your spouse can share together, why not start today? If you have the option of meeting your spouse for lunch or driving around paying utility bills so you'll save postage, ask yourself which of those activities is going to create a "moment"? Granted, saving postage is exciting, maybe even exhilarating, but a quiet lunch at some out-of-the-way bistro with the person you love can be even more exciting, and it'll make a great memory.

Moments—they can turn your marriage from ordinary to spectacular. Make sure you're planning plenty of them.

A Date to Communicate

Talk about a favorite moment in your married life.

Him:

Her:

What kind of a "moment" can you plan right now?

Him:

Her:

> After forty-five years of marriage, my husband, Charles, looks better to me now than he did in

our youth! I believe one of the secrets to our lasting marriage is that I found a man who loved God more than he did me.

Bev Lowry
Mother of comedian Mark Lowry

25

That Thing You Do

Knowing this, that the trying of your faith worketh patience.

James 1:3

THOSE qualities that first attracted you to your spouse will be the very same qualities that later drive you batty. That cute little giggle of hers that you used to love could become an irritating cackle after thirty years of marriage. His independent spirit, self-confident manner, and drive for success might, after a few decades of marital togetherness, be recategorized as "stubbornness, bull-headedness, and tunnel vision." Or maybe it was his command of the English language that originally attracted you to him. "He's such a terrific conversationalist. He can talk and talk and talk," you said back then. Now, after twenty years of marriage (and hearing the same stories 456 times), you might be saying, "All he ever does is *talk and talk and talk.* The guy hasn't taken a breath since he said 'I do'!"

When do those lovable qualities start turning into irritations? It can happen at any time. As far as why it happens, well, it could be that our spouses are aware of the things that first won our hearts, and in order to keep us interested, they think they've got to keep doing them, and doing them, and doing them. And when you look at it that way, maybe those qualities aren't so irritating after all.

A Date to Communicate

What quality or qualities first attracted you to your spouse?

Him:

Her:

Do you feel this is a quality that can be less than appealing if taken to the extreme?

Him:

Her:

> The secret to a good marriage is to have no secrets, i.e. put it all on the table, only AFTER you've eaten your dinner. Make sure you have a special dessert waiting and in sight; then you can talk, argue, if you must, but do settle it. Then have that dessert and make up!
>
> Andy Murcia
> Ann Jillian's husband/manager

26
Hold the Line

Set a watch, O LORD, before my mouth.

Psalm 141:3

Do you know that men and women view the telephone differently? I'm speaking in generalities, of course, but I think it's safe to say that most men don't consider the telephone receiver an accessory. Women, on the other hand, have a hard time feeling completely dressed without it. Maybe it's just me, but I see far more women using cell phones than men. I was at an airport once and watched a lady talking on her cellular while her husband deplaned, hugged his kids, hugged her, and walked on to get his luggage, leaving her behind, still talking on the phone.

I don't go to that extreme, but I have been known to have some pretty lengthy telephone conversations. We had a power outage not long ago and I talked another twenty minutes before even realizing the phone had gone dead. And thanks to the frequent flyer miles I earn for each minute I talk, I can now join John Glenn on his next space shuttle trip free of charge.

My husband is just the opposite. He hardly ever makes a call. And when he does, it's quick and to the point.

"Hi, how ya been? Fine? Good. Bye."

He's sincere, just concise.

But the telephone doesn't have to be a source of contention between a husband and wife. If both parties will try to understand each other's position on the matter, a suitable compromise can usually be reached. Like the one my husband and I reached not long ago. I'm going to try my best to hang up the phone once in a while and he's going to get my space shuttle ticket. There aren't any phones there anyway.

A Date to Communicate

Which one of you do you think spends more time on the telephone?

Him:

Her:

Has there ever been a time when you resented your spouse's time spent on the telephone? Talk it over.

Him:

Her:

> I was married by a judge. I should have asked for a jury.
>
> George Burns

27
To Your Corners, Please!

Behold, how good and how pleasant it is
for brethren to dwell together in unity!

Psalm 133:1

IN most marriages, there are disagreements. Whether it's over finances, the disciplining of children, the in-laws, or the proper way to hang the toilet paper, if you're married, chances are you're going to have your share of spats. There will be miscommunications, frustrating situations, and plenty of moments when you think your spouse comes from a planet a lot farther away than Venus or Mars.

I once read about a couple who had been married over seventy-five years. When asked for their secret to marital bliss, the husband answered, "Neither one of us can hear anymore, so it makes no sense to argue."

While we all have our own way of handling confrontations and disagreements, most of us fall into the following six categories:

First, there's the *pouter*. When confronted with a problem, the pouter will clam up and not say a single word, leaving the other party to fill in all the blanks. When the confused spouse dares to fill in a blank—incorrectly—the pouter will quickly break his or her silence with, "How could you say *that's* what I'm thinking?! You have no idea what I'm thinking!" And the pouter is right. Unless pouters actually *share* their feelings, there's no way for their spouses to know what's bothering them.

The *processor* is different than the pouter. Processors clam up as well, but they're not pouting. They're *processing*. Processors play the argument out in their heads, weighing the consequence of each sentence should they decide to speak. This assures the processor of having to eat only a minimal amount of words later. The problem with processors is they usually talk themselves out of saying what they really feel, and hence nothing much is ever solved.

The opposite of the pouter is the *shouter*. Shouters think their rightness is measured by their volume, so they use plenty of it. With shouters, it's hard to get a word in edgewise, so more often than not their spouses don't even try. This, unfortunately, gives shouters the misconception that they've won the argument, when all they've really done is intimidate any opposing view from ever being voiced.

The *"Did you say something, dear"* spouse basically "tunes out" his or her partner in all confrontational situations. Any other time they have perfect hearing, but let an uncomfortable topic come up and suddenly they need close captioning. It's a temporary condition, though, for once the matter is over, their hearing returns to normal and everything in *their* world is perfect again.

The *equalizer* is more than happy to accept blame, but not without bringing up one of her or his partner's infractions to "equalize" the situation. "I'll say I'm sorry, but only if you do." "I'll admit fault, but only if you admit some, too." "I'll make up, but you have to take the first step."

The *block wall* is just that—a block wall. They won't budge for anything. Nothing is their problem, their responsibility, or their concern.

Lastly, there's the *historian.* The historian doesn't complain at all. At least not at that moment. Historians simply file the entire incident into their memory banks for future retrieval. Months, even years from now, when you least expect it, they'll not only recall every detail of the ten-year-old infraction, but what the weather and stock reports were on that day as well.

Whether you fall into one of the above categories or have created a special one all your own, the most important thing to remember about settling any kind of disagreement is to listen, *really listen,* to what it is your partner is saying. You might be surprised to discover what's actually being said is completely different than what you're telling yourself you're hearing.

A Date to Communicate

Which category best describes how you handle disagreements?

Him:

Her:

In a disagreement, why do you think it's important to "listen" to your spouse's concerns?

Him:

Her:

Why do you think the Bible tells us not to let the sun go down on our wrath?

Him:

Her:

> Don't go to bed mad. Stay up and fight.
>
> Phyllis Diller

28
A Little Testy

Let us therefore follow after the things which make for peace, and things wherewith one may edify another.

Romans 14:19

"**WHAT'S** that you're doing?" my husband asked me one night.

"Filling out this questionnaire," I said.

"What kind of questionnaire?"

"It's supposed to tell us whether we have a happy marriage."

"We have a happy marriage."

"I know," I said. "I've got two copies. Wanna take it, too?"

"I don't need a test to tell me I'm happily married."

"C'mon," I said. "It'll be fun to see what kind of score we get."

That was the last civil word we exchanged that entire evening. As near as I can recall, the conversation went something like this:

Me: *(reading from test)* "What's the one thing about your spouse that irritates you the most?"

He: I'm not going to answer that question.

Me: You have to.

He: No, I don't. You said this was just for fun.

Me: Right. And you're not making it any fun.

He: Remaining alive would be fun.

Me: This is just a simple little test. You can answer honestly.

He: All right. *That's* what irritates me the most about you.

Me: What's that?

He: That you won't leave well enough alone. Next question.

Me: We can't go on to the next question until you explain that last answer.

He: I gave you an answer, now let's move on.

Me: Oh, all right, next question. What's the . . . *what do you mean I won't leave well enough alone?*

He: You're doing it right now.

Me: I am not.

He: You are too. Anyway, how did *you* answer that question? What'd you say was the most irritating thing about me?

Me: That was easy. You're always finishing my sentences.

He: No, I'm not.

Me: Yes, you are. You're always . . .

He: . . . finishing your sentences? That's absurd!

Me: You just did it.

He: Did what?

Me: Finished my . . .

He: . . . sentence? You're just saying that because you couldn't think of anything else.

Me: I'm saying it because it's true.

He: Well, then, how'd you answer question #6? The one about my best quality?

Me: I skipped that.

He: You *skipped* it?

Me: You have *so many* good qualities, dear, I didn't know which one to pick.

He: Try.

Me: I'll come back to it.

He: I wrote yours down.

Me: What'd you say?

He: Tell me my best quality first.

Me: Okay. Your sense of humor.

He: My sense of humor? What about my good looks?

Me: Your sense of humor isn't thinning on top.

And it continued downhill from there. I sometimes wonder how many divorces have been filed after a happily married couple took a test to see whether they were happily married.

Tests can be fun. Some may even help you better understand yourself and your mate. But only the two of you can determine whether yours is a good marriage or one that needs a little extra attention. And if it's the latter, only the two of you can make sure it gets it.

A Date to Communicate

How would *you* answer the question "What's your mate's best quality?"

His answer:

Her answer:

Do you feel your marriage could use a little extra attention? In what areas?

His answer:

Her answer:

> A simple philosophy is the key to our twenty-seven-year marriage . . . keep your eye upon the doughnut, and not upon the hole. In other words, nobody's perfect. There are plenty of days when I want to see my husband's body outlined in chalk, and vice versa. But it's our choice as to whether we'll dwell on what's driving us nuts about the other person, or dwell on what's right with the other person.
>
> Kathy Peel
> Founder and chairman,
> Family Manager, Inc.

29

Who's Minding the Vacuum?

She looketh well to the ways of her household, and eateth not the bread of idleness.

Proverbs 31:27

He also that is slothful in his work is
brother to him that is a great waster.

Proverbs 18:9

THE distribution of household chores can be
a real source of contention for married couples.
A wife may think her husband shouldn't have to
be told to pick up after himself or mow the lawn.
A husband may believe a wife should change the

sheets long before the floral pattern starts taking root.

I'll admit my kitchen could use a little attention. It's decorated in teal and salmonella, and there's milk in my refrigerator that's been there so long, we give it birthday parties. Don't get me wrong. I'm not saying my home is a toxic waste site, but Mr. Clean did have a full head of hair before he started disinfecting my sink.

But in this day of Mr. Moms and Ms. Dads, who does which household chore has little to do with your sex. More often than not, it simply falls on who's available. Whether you're a husband helping with the dishes or a wife changing the oil in the family car, what really matters about household chores isn't who's doing them, but that they get done.

To help you know whether it's time for one or both of you to start paying a little more attention to the house, ask yourself the following questions:

Have you ever caught your kids playing soccer in the house using a dust ball?

Does your washing machine need a mildew cycle?

Do you find your dinner guests licking their plates clean *before* the meal?

Is your kitchen floor so sticky, you pull up the linoleum every time you take a step?

When your neighbors put trash in its place, do they bring it over to your house?

Is there a "no vacancy" sign hanging outside your roach motel?

Does your Airwick Solid melt fifteen minutes after you put it out?

Are the cobwebs at your house so big, you use them for a volleyball net?

Does your no-pest strip need a control tower?

Has your home ever qualified for a disaster loan without the inconvenience of a disaster?

If your answer is "yes" to any of the above, maybe it's time to sit down and start dividing up the chores. After all, a man's home may be his castle, but it shouldn't look like horses run through it on a regular basis.

A Date to Communicate

Name a single household chore that you'd love for your spouse to take care of this week.

Him:

Her:

Name one thing about your housekeeping or yard work that you feel could use some improvement.

Him:

Her:

> I'm so lazy, the only way to get me out of bed in the morning is to put helium in my pajamas.
>
> Bob Hope
> Family Manager, Inc.

30
When I Want Your Opinion . . .

Be kindly affectioned one to another with brotherly love; in honour preferring one another.

Romans 12:10

MY parents had a mixed marriage—my mother was a Republican, my father was a Democrat. It didn't matter to them that every time they voted, they were just canceling each other out. They were voicing their opinion, and that was the important thing.

I benefited from my parents being independent thinkers. There were healthy discussions about a lot of things in the news. Even when they had opposing viewpoints, I can't recall them ever arguing over them. They respected each other's opinion and cherished their right to voice that opinion.

As far as I know, they never missed an election. Often they'd make it to their precinct just before closing time, but they'd make it. They believed their vote counted, even when the winners were announced by East Coast newscasters before the polls had closed in the west.

I appreciate the example my parents set of mutually respecting one another's opinions. That's important in a marriage. When the Bible says "the two shall become one," it doesn't mean that they will always think and act exactly alike. A marriage is a team—two people working together for the ultimate good of the unit. Each partner brings different life experiences, a variety of talents, and, yes, sometimes opposing opinions to the table. Respect those differences. You wouldn't really want to marry a clone of yourself, or have clones for children, would you? Sure, everyone would think exactly like you do, but let's face it, it'd make for some pretty boring family portraits.

A Date to Communicate

What are some issues that you and your spouse have differing opinions on?

Him:

Her:

Even though you disagree, why do you think it's important to respect one another's opinions?

Him:

Her:

> Whoever said that marriage was a 50–50 proposition had either a great marriage or a terrible sense of proportions.
>
> Gene Perret
> Comedy writer

34
Perfect Timing

He that is of a proud heart stirreth up strife.

Proverbs 28:25

TIMING. Good comedy depends on it. So does a marriage. It's important that marriage partners be open and honest with each other about their feelings. Honest assessments are the only way proper adjustments can be made. But there's a right time and a wrong time to do this.

The day your husband gets laid off from work and has to fight bumper-to-bumper traffic for two hours getting home would not be a good time to insist on your night out with your friends.

When your wife spends all night nursing your three-year-old's ear infection, then spends all afternoon in the principal's office discussing why your third-grader rode the ceiling fan in the school cafeteria, that probably wouldn't be a good time to continue that discussion about having more children.

What you want to say may be perfectly in order. Your complaints might be valid and your argument persuasive, but if your timing is off, you're not going to be heard.

Common sense tells you that if your spouse is already having a bad day, he or she needs encouragement, not criticism. If the matter can wait, hold on to it for a while. You can always bring it up later. And sometimes, if you wait long enough, the problem starts looking a whole lot smaller, or better yet, it ends up going away altogether.

A Date to Communicate

When you have a problem that you need to discuss with your spouse, do you feel you use good timing in presenting it?

131

Him:

Her:

How do you feel when someone presents a problem on a day when you're already stressed to your limit?

Him:

Her:

> Two words that should be eliminated from marital arguments: "never" and "always" (as in "you NEVER . . ." or "you ALWAYS . . ."). Get rid of those and you'll have a reasonable chance of fighting fairly and productively.
>
> Paul McCusker
> Writer

132

32
The Impossible?

Behold, thou desireth truth in the inward parts.

Psalm 51:6

WALKING along a California beach one night, a man came upon an old lamp nestled by the rocks. When he picked it up and rubbed it, a genie suddenly appeared.

"All right, that's it!" snapped the genie. "This is the fourth time this month someone's disturbed me! I'm so mad I'm only going to grant you one wish instead of three! So, come on, come on! Tell me what is it you want, and don't take all day!"

The man thought it over quickly, then said, "Well, I've always dreamed of going to Hawaii, but I have a fear of flying and I tend to get seasick on boats. How about if you build me a bridge to Hawaii? That way, I can just drive there."

The genie laughed. "A bridge to Hawaii?! You've got to be kidding! How would I get the supports to reach the bottom of the ocean? That'd take way too much steel, far too much concrete! It simply can't be done! Think of another wish!"

Disappointed, the man tried his best to think of another wish. Finally, he said, "All right, I've got one. All the women in my life say I'm insensitive. I try and try to please them, but nothing works. I don't know what I'm doing wrong. My one wish is to understand women . . . know what they're really feeling when they're giving me the silent treatment . . . know why it is they're crying . . . know what it is they want when they're not telling me what it is they want. . . . I want to know how to make them truly happy."

There was a slight pause, then the genie said, "You want that bridge two lanes or four?"

Source unknown

All right, I admit it. The above joke leaves the impression that women are hard to understand.

But by the laughter it receives whenever it's told, there must be some truth to it.

The main reason that understanding women is such a difficult task is that we don't always make our desires and needs clear. We tell our husbands that we don't want to do anything big for our anniversaries, then pout for three weeks because they didn't plan anything big. We say we'll be happy to cook dinner even though we'd really rather go out to eat, then we grumble and complain during the entire meal about how tired we are and that no one cares. We're hard to understand because we often send conflicting messages.

Wouldn't it be better for everyone if we'd just say what we really want? We might decide not to do anything big for our anniversary anyway, we might still cook dinner instead of going out to eat, but at least we will have properly communicated our true desires. Our spouses will know where we're really coming from, and we'll feel better about it, too.

A Date to Communicate

Is there something coming up that you'd really like to do, but have communicated something else to your spouse?

Him:

Her:

Why do you think it's important to always communicate your true feelings to each other?

Him:

Her:

> Quarrels never could last long,
> If on one side only lay the wrong.
> Benjamin Franklin

33
They're Playing Our Song

Make sweet melody, sing many songs.

Isaiah 23:16

IF you're like most couples, you have a song that you call your own, a song that fills your hearts with memories every time you hear it. It could be the song that was being played when you first laid eyes on each other, as is the case with Bob and Dolores Hope.

When Bob first saw Dolores, she was on stage at the *Vogue Club* on 57th Street in New York singing "Paper Moon." So smitten was he of this

Irish/Italian beauty that he invited her to come see him perform across town in the Broadway musical, *Roberta*. Wanting to encourage this handsome, struggling young actor who probably had barely one or two lines, she went, having no idea that he was one of the leads. They began dating, eventually married, and over the next sixty-six-plus years the two of them have never forgotten "their song."

Maybe your song dates back to your very first encounter, or perhaps it's one that helped bring the two of you through a particularly rough time in your lives. Or maybe it's the song that was sung at your wedding, or one that was popular when your first child was born. It doesn't matter how or why a song becomes your song. The important thing is that it's yours.

Whatever song you claim as your own, from Lee Greenwood's "I Owe You" to Shania Twain's "From This Moment" to that romantic country classic, "You're the Reason Our Kids Are Ugly," it's important for couples to have their own song. If you don't have one, why not take a moment right now to discuss what song best describes your relationship together. Then, whenever you hear that song played, you'll think of each other whether you're rooms apart or oceans apart. It'll be your song.

A Date to Communicate

What is your song?

Why does this particular song mean something special to the two of you?

Him:

Her:

> From day one I felt indebted to him because he always did so much for me. I wanted to do as much for him.
>
> Wanda Rider
> Teacher, writer
> Married forty years

34

Prayer Partners

The LORD is nigh unto all them that call upon him.

Psalm 145:18

THE church has always been a very important part of our married life. My husband and I met in church, most of our dates were church events, and we both ended up working in the church and raising our three sons in church. In fact, some of our closest friends to this day came out of the first church we attended as a young married couple.

There is a lot of talk these days about the importance of communication in a marriage, the importance of the marriage bed, and the importance of mutual respect, while all too often the spiritual aspect of a relationship is overlooked.

It's a good, healthy thing when a couple can share a spiritual life together. There's an unparalleled closeness that develops when a couple prays together, when they share God's Word with their children, and when they are an active part of a church family.

A Date to Communicate

How often do you and your spouse pray together?

What do you think are some benefits that would come from you and your spouse enjoying a richer spiritual life together?

Him:

Her:

There are three of us in this marriage—God, Corrine, and I. The closer we get to God individually, the closer we get to each other.

Robert Hanley
Actor

35
Addictions

O Israel, thou hast destroyed thyself; but in me is thine help.

Hosea 13:9

MY father didn't have a gambling problem. He didn't have a drinking problem. My father wasn't seeing another woman behind my mother's back. His addiction didn't have a twelve-step program to help empower him to overcome it. His addiction was grocery shopping.

Every payday, my mother would round up all five of us kids and go to the local Dale's grocery store to track down my father before he had the chance to spend his entire paycheck on canned goods. Canned goods were his greatest weakness,

143

and that's where we'd usually find him. He'd be there by the Del Monte shelf, filling his shopping cart so full of canned vegetables, he could barely push it. Mom would sneak up behind him and catch him redhanded holding a six-pack of turnip greens or getting ready to overdose on cans of sliced beets. As soon as he saw her, he'd sheepishly try to explain his actions. He'd say things like, "But they're on sale," or "You never know when there's going to be a beet shortage!" Mom would see right through him, though, and start unloading the basket, saving him from himself while explaining why we needed that money for other things, like the monthly bills.

My dad was always good-natured about it, and those Friday night grocery store stakeouts will always be a beloved part of my childhood memories.

Some couples have to deal with addictions that are far more serious, though. Drinking, drugs, gambling, and out-of-control spending habits are behaviors that can rip a family apart. If you and your partner are dealing with unhealthy addictions, the best advice is to seek professional help as soon as possible. With proper counseling, you can recognize the reasons behind your destructive pattern of behavior and be on the road to

144

overcoming it. Ignore the behavior and you're running the risk of it eventually overcoming you.

A Date to Communicate

Are you struggling with a certain behavior that you know is detrimental to your marriage?

Him:

Her:

In what ways has this behavior already hurt your relationship?

Him:

Her:

> Nothing so needs reforming as other people's habits.
>
> Mark Twain

36
Driving Me Batty

For thou art my rock and my fortress;
therefore for thy name's sake lead me, and
guide me.

Psalm 31:3

MEN have been accusing women of backseat
driving for years, but no one's better at backseat
driving than my husband. He's always giving me
advice.

"Watch out for that tree!"

"Stay off the sidewalk!"

"That was no speed bump. It was a planter!"

146

Nag, nag, nag, nag, nag. He offers more travel instructions than the Automobile Club. I'm sure he thinks men are better drivers than women.

But I beg to differ. I'd like to see a man try to parallel park while applying mascara, or maneuver through three lanes of traffic while changing from dress shoes to Reeboks. A man couldn't execute a perfect three-point turn while refereeing three six-year-olds in the back seat, or merge onto a freeway while applying lip liner with the precision of a skilled draftsman.

Women have these skills down pat.

In the long run, though, it doesn't really matter which sex is the better driver. What matters is whose directions you're *both* following in life—yours, your spouse's, or God's?

A Date to Communicate

Who would you say is in the driver's seat in your marriage?

His answer:

Her answer:

Why do you think it's important to let God be in control?

Him:

Her:

> My wife loves to argue. When I said, " I do," she said, " Oh, no you don't!"
>
> Gene Perret

37

Stop and Smell the Roses

I thank my God upon every remembrance of you.

Philippians 1:3

WHEN my husband and I were dating, he began a tradition of sending roses to me every month on the anniversary of our first date. They were long-stemmed red ones and they'd be delivered to my house in a gold, oblong box. For our fourteen-month anniversary, he sent fourteen roses; our twenty-three-month anniversary, twenty-three roses; and so on. They usually arrived while I was at school and my grandmother, Ella Stevens, would take them out of the box and arrange them in a vase. I honestly believe she looked forward to their arrival as much as I did. Each month, she'd mark the date on her calendar and spend that day watching out the window for the florist's van.

Three-and-a-half years of dating and forty-two roses later, we decided to marry. (I think he figured it'd be a whole lot cheaper!) To this day, though, my husband still brings me flowers, only now they're wildflowers that he picks alongside of the road as he's finishing his daily jog.

Some good friends of ours, Jim and Ginger Forester, have bought a special ornament every Christmas since their wedding day. Not only is their Christmas tree each year one of the prettiest you'll ever see, but it's filled with loving, cherished memories.

Another married couple I know go away for "weekend honeymoons" as often as they can. These little getaways help them refocus on their marriage and on each other.

Whether it's weekend trips, flowers, ornaments, going to a favorite restaurant on a special "date night," putting love notes in his lunch, cooking breakfast for her on Saturday morning, or going for Sunday afternoon drives, traditions are important in a marriage. They remind us of those wonderful feelings of yesterday and keep us looking forward to the future together.

A Date to Communicate

Is there a tradition that you and your spouse have started?

Him:

Her:

What new tradition would you like to begin this week?

Him:

Her:

A good marriage is shaped by sacred vows. Renewing our vows every ten years has kept the promises fresh in our minds and in our lives. On July 1, 2000, God willing, they will turn golden.

Diantha Ain
Writer, composer

38

This Meeting Is Called to Order

For this God is our God for ever and ever:
he will be our guide even unto death.

Psalm 48:14

"WHEN are you going to learn to plan ahead?!"

"I do plan ahead."

"No, you don't. You brought the car home on empty again. How is *that* planning ahead?"

"I planned for *you* to fill it up in the morning."

It's good to plan ahead, to set goals, to ask yourselves where you want to be as a couple five, ten, or even twenty years from now. Goals give you something to aim for and, hopefully, reach.

Once, while on a trip to the south when my husband and I were at a particular crossroads in our lives, he called the desk clerk at the hotel where we were staying and asked for an easel and posterboard to be brought to our room.

When the bewildered bellhop delivered the items, my husband tipped him, closed the door, then proceeded to conduct a meeting right there by the in-room coffeemaker on the five-year Bolton plan. He wrote down our long-term goals, our short-term goals, how those goals line up with God's will for our lives, and what obstacles we might have to overcome to meet those goals. I have to admit it was a little strange, especially since he made me raise my hand every time I wanted to comment, but in retrospect that meeting was a great idea. It got us back on course, and helped us reevaluate our priorities and plan our future with the "big picture" in mind.

One certain fact about life is that we're all going to be thrown some curves. That's a given. But a prayerful, well-thought-out plan can keep those curves from tripping us up, getting us off course, and causing us to lose sight of and ultimately surrender our goals.

A Date to Communicate

What are your short-term goals?

Him:

Her:

What are your long-term goals?

Him:

Her:

What obstacles will you have to overcome to meet these goals?

Him:

Her:

Have you prayed about these goals?

Him:

Her:

> The Grecian ladies counted their age from their marriage, not their birth.
>
> Homer
> (probably not a bad idea)

39
Best of Friends

A friend loveth at all times.

Proverbs 17:17

IF your spouse isn't your best friend, he or she should be high on the list. But what is it that makes a friend?

A friend sees the best in you, even when you're not showing it.

A friend knows when you need someone to talk to, when you need to be alone, and, most important, the difference between the two.

157

A friend can tell when you need a hug, and doesn't hesitate to offer one.

A friend makes you laugh when you see little to laugh about.

A friend will always come to your defense, no matter how often called upon to do it or how unpopular it makes her or him.

A friend believes you first and rumors second.

A friend never passes up the chance to encourage you.

A friend shares with you, even chocolate.

A friend tells you when you're about to make a mistake.

A friend is someone you can always depend on, even when you don't deserve it.

A friend brings out the best in you, but doesn't insist on the credit.

A friend understands you, even when you don't.

A friend makes the best spouse.

A Date to Communicate

Do you feel you and your spouse are best friends? Why or why not?

158

His answer:

Her answer:

Why do you think friendship is important in a marriage?

His answer:

Her answer:

> Marriage is a mystery . . . the attempted merger of two minds aided and abetted by the certain merger of two hearts.
>
> Linda Aleahmad
> Psychotherapist

40
Such a Deal

For the love of money is the root of all evil:
which while some coveted after, they have
erred from the faith, and pierced themselves through with many sorrows.

1 Timothy 6:10

IF I were to take a poll among married couples, most would probably confess to having had
this experience at least once in their married life.
A salesperson, friend, co-worker, or even a fel-

low church member managed to talk them into some sort of get-rich-quick scheme that not only didn't bring them their fortune, but took a good chunk out of what they already had.

Encyclopedias, household products, stock investments, real estate ventures—these get-rich-quick schemes come in all shapes and sizes. Some may be legitimate, but many aren't, and if you're not careful, they can leave you wishing you had followed Nancy Reagan's drug abuse advice and "just said no."

After being stung a few times, you start learning to tell your long-time best friend or, more often than not, your brand-new "best friend" to go ahead and make the first million, then come and ask you to join up.

We almost learned our lesson the hard way in the early years of our marriage. Our salesman/friend wanted us to invest three thousand dollars in a company he had just joined. According to him, it was a virtually risk-free operation because we'd get three thousand dollars of soap to keep in our garage in exchange for our cash investment. Then, if we didn't make any money, we'd still have the soap. I guess he figured we could sell it door-to-door or give it away as Christmas presents.

We got close to biting the bait, but decided against it at the last minute. We found out later that our friend ended up losing all of his investment—thousands of dollars. But he still had his soap.

You would have thought we'd learn from that experience, but over the years we've had more. We're frequently trapped into those "free" time share vacations where all you have to do is listen to a salesperson pitch the time share. The vacations are nice, but often the sales pitch is so high pressure, the only way out of the room is to either buy into the time share or fake a heart attack. We've tried the latter, but the salesperson just tells us to keep it down and continues with the slide presentation.

As much as we'd like to believe otherwise, most of us are probably not going to get rich overnight. The best plan for financial well-being is hard work, wise spending choices, and deliberate saving. So don't let the pressure of friends or strangers cause you to make risky decisions about your money. They may be absolutely convinced they're going to strike it rich, and they might. But make sure they're not accumulating their wealth by taking yours. Friend or not.

A Date to Communicate

Have you had an experience similar to the above?

What do you think is the best way to achieve financial independence?

His answer:

Her answer:

> Our marriage was made in heaven—which also happens to be where God makes thunder and lightning. I tend to be the bright flash and he's the deep boom— quite opposite, but somehow we go together nicely.
>
> Robin Jones Gunn
> Author, speaker
> Married over twenty years

44

A House Divided

A talebearer revealeth secrets, but he that is of a faithful spirit, concealeth the matter.

Proverbs 11:13

KNOW people who gladly expound on every shortcoming of their spouses? They'll tell you about his jealousy, her temper, his snoring, and her spending habits. You learn about the year he forgot to buy her a birthday gift, and the time she backed out of the garage without the convenience of the garage door being open.

Couples who tear each other down often don't realize the long-term ramifications of their actions. Not much good can be accomplished on a team where the players aren't working together. If a basketball player badmouthed his teammates to opposing teams, if he told about all their vulnerabilities, if he sabotaged every play they attempted, it wouldn't take long for the team to fall apart.

Like basketball, marriage is a team effort. If one or both parties gets on the telephone to friends or extended family and keeps everyone updated with a minute-by-minute account of every disagreement or misunderstanding, it's not healthy. Why? The outside parties are only getting one side of the story and, therefore, can't always offer the best advice. The outside parties aren't qualified to offer the best advice. And lastly, the outside parties may be offering advice for their own interest and not for the good of your marriage.

Be a team player when it comes to your marriage. If you have genuine problems, talk it over with a counselor, minister, or some other professional who can offer sound advice. Otherwise, instead of tearing down your husband or wife to others, build your partner up. Gossip, if you must, about the good qualities. Then when something you say gets back to your spouse—and in time it will—she or he will feel loved, not betrayed.

A Date to Communicate

When you talk about your spouse to others, are you building up or tearing down?

Him:

Her:

How do you want your spouse to talk about you when with friends?

Him:

Her:

Prepare for the home stretch.
Bob Hope
Married sixty-six years

42
Name That Wife

Let all those that put their trust in thee rejoice: let them shout for joy.

Psalm 5:11

MY husband has a variety of pet names for me. I don't know how he comes up with these names (too much caffeine must have something to do with it), but it can get a little embarrassing when he's introducing me to his business associates.

"Captain Buchanan, I'd like you to meet my wife, Honey Biscuit."

"Reverend Salsota, this is my wife, Love Bumps."

"Sugar Bear, this is Congresswoman Stafford. Congresswoman Stafford, this is Sugar Bear."

It wouldn't be so bad, but that's how he fills out my name tags, too.

Still, pet names can add a little fun to your marriage. They're something that you, and only you, call your spouse. (Although, an insurance salesman called our house the other day asking to speak with Love Bumps.)

Pet names are an endearing expression of love. Sure, they can be embarrassing, but when I think about all the names some husbands call their wives and vice versa, *Honey Biscuit* doesn't sound all that bad.

But now, *Passion Petunia?* You've just got to draw the line somewhere!

A Date to Communicate

What are some of your pet names for your spouse?

Him:

Her:

Why do you think it's important to have fun with your spouse?

Him:

Her:

> My secret to a happy marriage is laughter.
>
> Debbie Christesson
> Teacher, mother, wife,
> former missionary

43
Shall We Gather at the Thermostat

Let us therefore follow after the things
which make for peace, and things wherewith one may edify another.

Romans 14:19

THE cold war has been over for some time.
But that's *that* cold war. There's another one
raging at our house, and its front line is the
thermostat!

You've heard of the War of 1812? This is the
War of 76 . . . degrees, that is. My husband thinks
76 is the optimum thermostat setting. I, on the
other hand, prefer to set it a little higher than

that—like somewhere between the 80-degree mark and "Volcano."

My feet tend to run the coldest. The only time in our marriage that my husband hasn't complained about my cold feet rubbing up against his legs was when he sprained his ankle and said my icy toes were making the swelling go down.

Our temperature conflict spills over into the car as well. My husband could be driving through a blizzard and he'll still roll down his window and open the vent. I'm the extreme opposite. Whenever I drive, I want the windows airtight and the heater turned up to its highest setting, at least until we finish crossing the desert.

The problem is my husband actually believes he's a thermostat. He must. No matter how many people are in the house, car, room, store, or restaurant, my husband thinks he's the only one who knows the true temperature of the area and what needs to be done to adjust it. If he's cold, it's cold. If he's hot, it's hot. Never mind that he's wearing a wool suit and just drank three cups of steaming hot coffee. He's hot, so America's hot.

This Battle of the Thermostat has been going on since our honeymoon (I wore the veil to bed so I wouldn't catch a head cold), and it's a long way from ever getting solved. So in the meantime, I guess he'll have to sleep in front of the air conditioner and I'll just have to keep wearing my parka to bed. It's a workable compromise. I just wish my snowshoes would quit getting snagged on the blankets.

A Date to Communicate

What is your ideal temperature setting?

Him:

Her:

List ways that you can compromise to reach a satisfactory room temperature for the both of you.

Him:

Her:

In our marriage we've learned: (1) There are more important things than being right. (2) A sense of humor can help you survive just about anything. For example, at an early age Sandy had a hysterectomy and we cannot have children. When questioned by well-meaning people as to why we don't have children, we simply tell them, "God wouldn't let us breed." (No way He's dipping in that gene pool!) (3) As a result, when problems arise, rather than find fault with each other, we simply blame it on our imaginary children! Or inanimate objects. Nearly everything in our house can talk . . . or argue. On the downside, we end up breaking a lot of our inanimate objects.

Denny and Sandy Brownlee
Writers, performers,
radio personalities
Married fifteen years

44

Embarrassing Moments

I know both how to be abased, and I know how to abound.

Philippians 4:12

EMBARRASSING moments—what would a marriage be without them?

The other day while we were pumping gas at a nearby station, a man and his wife pulled up to pump #6 several islands away. They were in a brand-new Lexus, which made us turn and notice. Things like that stand out when you're filling up an '88 Ford T-bird with no air conditioning and windows that won't roll down.

174

The man got out, sauntered over to the station, then returned to pump his gas. His wife, basking in the attention they both were receiving, held her head high and patiently waited for him to fill up their tank. Today, however, it was going to take a little longer than usual.

"Pump #6," the voice bellowed over the speakers at each pump. "Your credit card was rejected. Come inside to pay cash!"

The man tried to maintain his dignity as he looked at his wife and they exchanged those glares that every married couple knows all too well. Those looks that say, "I thought you paid the bill." "I thought you paid the bill." "You said you were going to pay it!" "You always pay the bills. Why would I pay it?!"

Children provide plenty of embarrassing moments, too. Like the time we were vacationing in Palm Springs. Our children, about two, two, and four years of age, were thoroughly enjoying the motel wading pool. They were the only ones in it and having the time of their lives. I was, too, until one of them said that he had to go to the restroom. So, telling my husband to watch the other two boys, I walked him all the way down the hall, up the stairs, and back to our room.

After taking care of business, we walked down the stairs, down the hall, and back out to the pool. By now, though, one of his brothers needed to go. So, back down the hall I went, child in tow, up the stairs, and back to our room.

He, too, took care of business and we returned to the pool where, yep, you guessed it, the third one had to go. Not wanting to climb the stairs again, and knowing that he had a swim diaper on, I whispered for him to just go on and go in the pool. He looked at me like I had lost my mind, then shrugged as if to say, "Okay, Mom, if you say so."

I laid back and tried to resume my sunbathing, but as I did, I caught a glimpse of something unusual out of the corner of my eye. I turned in his direction and there he was, standing by the side of the pool, swim suit and diaper both down at his ankles, and, like a fountain, he was "going in the pool."

This time, my husband took him to the bathroom. Embarrassing moments. You want to die at the time, but they bring you a lot of laughter. And, like oil in a car, laughter is something every marriage needs. Without it, all you'll get is friction and sparks.

176

A Date to Communicate

What was your most embarrassing moment? Talk about it.

Him:

Her:

Is it something you can laugh at today? Why or why not?

Him:

Her:

> Nothing is important a month later.
>
> Will Rogers

45
Mismatched

Fulfil ye my joy, that ye be likeminded, having the same love, being of one accord, of one mind.

Philippians 2:2

My husband and I never dress like we're going to the same function. He prefers to dress down (for him, jogging shorts and a tucked-in T-shirt is formal attire). I, on the other hand, tend to overdress. I once played a Little League game in a semiformal and high heels. Not on purpose. I had a banquet to attend after my son's game, but since the other team didn't show up and the kids suggested playing against the parents, well . . . let's just say sliding into first base never looked so elegant.

I know my husband and I aren't the only mismatched couple. I've seen plenty of men in bermuda shorts walking arm in arm with women in pearls and chiffon. That's because most men think of comfort first, while most women consider their appearance more important.

There are some advantages to mismatched dressing, though. If we get a flat tire on our way to a function, it's obvious which one of us is dressed to change it. By the same token, if we happen to run into the Queen of England at Kroger's, I will be the one who gets to approach her in the frozen food aisle, not him.

There are some couples who dress totally alike. They wear matching shirts, matching shorts and socks, sometimes even a matching hat. This makes for some fun pictures and no doubt helps them find each other in a crowded room, but I don't think that idea would work for my husband and me. I mean, which look could we agree on? I'm far too pale to ever wear shorts in public and he just doesn't look all that good in pearls.

A Date to Communicate

Do you consider yourself a casual dresser or more formal?

Him:

Her:

Is there an article of clothing that you wish your spouse would replace? Why do you think your spouse enjoys wearing it so much?

Him:

Her:

My secret to a happy marriage?
1. Marriage is a work in progress (and you do work at it).

2. Respect and love go hand in hand. So many essential elements in a marriage are fueled by respect—understanding, compassion, patience, longsuffering, etc., etc.

3. "Love thy neighbor as thyself." Christ directed us to do so. Note: He also said "thyself," so . . . loving, respecting ourselves, and working at it helps us to love and respect each other.

Ann Jillian
Actress

46
The Lost Boys

Lead me in thy truth, and teach me.

Psalm 25:5

I don't know why men hate to admit it when they're lost, but it's a common problem for those of the male gender. Not that *all* men suffer from this affliction, but enough of them do to warrant a chapter on the condition.

My husband has a severe case of it, but he's in denial. Just this week he drove hundreds of miles out of our way just because he refused to stop and ask directions. We passed six Texaco stations, eight Mobil stations, four Shell stations, and a two-story Information Center, yet he kept on driving, waiting for "something to look familiar." We'd still be out there touring the country, if he didn't hit the edge of the Grand Canyon and was forced to turn around.

I'm sure I'm not the only wife who's planned for a vacation in one state only to end up in another. That's why I've provided the following:

Diary of a Lost Male

10 minutes lost	"I know *exactly* where I'm going."
20 minutes lost	"It's around this next bend. I'm sure of it."
30 minutes lost	"Stop and ask directions? Why? I know this road like the back of my hand!"
40 minutes lost	"See, I told you. It's right up ahead."
50 minutes lost	"They moved it! *Can you believe that? They moved it!*"
1 hour lost	"Give me five more minutes, then I'll stop and ask someone."
1–1/2 hours lost	"We are *not* going in circles! I'm just doubling back to make sure I didn't pass it."
2 hours lost	"All right, all right. I'll stop at the next gas station and ask directions. But we're only wasting time."

2–1/2 hours lost	"Now it's *my* fault all the gas stations are closed? *I* didn't tell them to close."
3 hours lost	"Things are starting to look familiar now. I think we're close."
3–1/2 hours lost	"I think we're lost."
4 hours lost	"Maybe we'd better get a room for the night. We'll be able to see the street signs better in the morning."
The next morning	"Wake up! Let's hit the road! I just remembered how to get there! . . . Map? *Who needs a map?*"

A Date to Communicate

If we know that asking for directions ahead of time is going to save us stress and perhaps even an argument, why do you think we don't do it?

His answer:

Her answer:

Why do you think it's important to always follow God's directions in our marriages?

His answer:

Her answer:

We've been holding hands for fifty years . . . 'cause if we let go, we'd kill each other.

Betty Bergenthal
Housewife
Married fifty-four years

47
Empty Nest

Lo, children are an heritage of the LORD.
Psalm 127:3

BECAUSE our sons are so close in age, the empty nest syndrome hit my husband and me all at once. It took a lot of adjustment. All of a sudden it was just the two of us again. No more cooking dinner for the whole family. Now I only had two servings of food to burn instead of five.

Our water bill went down, the noise level went down, our food bill went down, our car insurance went down, and our spirits took a nose dive.

Sure, we could use the telephone whenever we wanted. We could stay in the bathroom as long as we wanted. And we didn't have to tell anyone to turn down the stereo. It was so quiet around the house, we both thought we'd gone deaf. It was quiet and peaceful—and we hated it.

Kids grow up too fast. If you've got a two-year-old hanging onto your leg and you're chasing the twin five-year-olds down the hallway trying to get them into the bathtub, you're probably wishing they'd grow up *now*. But trust me, it'll happen soon enough. Before you know it, you'll be sitting in a church pew watching them exchange wedding vows. You'll be seeing them hold their own baby. You'll be visiting with a man or a woman instead of your little boy or girl. You'll be missing that child you once had and wishing you had the noise back for just one day.

So, if you're a parent, enjoy every minute of your parenting years. You only get one pass at it. Make it everything it can be.

A Date to Communicate

If you have children, what is your favorite memory of each of them?

Him:

Her:

What can you do today to slow down and enjoy the parenting years even more?

Him:

Her:

> The secret to a happy marriage?
> Communication and a lot of love.
>> Tommy and Jean Thompson
>> Married fifty-seven years

48
R-E-S-P-E-C-T

Honour shall uphold the humble in spirit.
Proverbs 29:23

ACCORDING to the familiar Aretha Franklin song, R-E-S-P-E-C-T is an important part of a relationship. It's especially crucial in a marriage.

Have you ever spent an evening with a husband and wife who didn't show any respect for each other? She snaps at him. He barks at her. The entire evening is an endless stream of putdowns and nitpicking—from his terrible driving habits to her out of control shopping sprees, from his poor choice in restaurants to her controlling personality. They pass the evening verbally beating each other up and you have a ringside seat, whether you want it or not.

Respect isn't something that can be faked. It doesn't matter how many times you say you respect your spouse. If your actions are demonstrating a lack of respect, you're not fooling anyone.

It's important to note, though, that respect isn't fear. Don't mistake the two. Respect comes from a place of honor. It's admiration, not intimidation.

Respect shouldn't be something you use as a bargaining tool, either. It shouldn't be tied to the balance in your checkbook or to your spouse's latest failure. Respect, if real, will be present regardless of circumstances. We respect our spouses because of who we know they are inside, who we know they can become, and because of the position they hold within the family.

R-E-S-P-E-C-T. Make sure it's the real thing.

A Date to Communicate

Do you feel you show your spouse enough respect?

Him:

Her:

Name three reasons why your spouse is worthy of your respect.

Him:

Her:

> The compliment that helps us on our way is not the one that is shut up in the mind, but the one that is spoken out.
>
> Mark Twain

49

What Date Was That Again?

Have fervent charity among yourselves:
for charity shall cover the multitude of sins.

1 Peter 4:8

I once read about a man who got married on his birthday. That way, he figured, he'd never forget his anniversary. Smart guy. We live with the threat of international terrorism, El Niño, catastrophic earthquakes, killer tornadoes and hurricanes, but no terror matches that of a forgotten anniversary.

We don't mean to forget. We just get busy. The kids have to be taken to Little League games, piano practice, scout meetings. We mark the special day on our calendars, highlight it in our day planners, and post notes all over the house, then forget to look at any of them. The next thing we know our spouse is waking us up at 11:59 P.M. informing us that we have just one minute left to produce a card, flowers, gift, or some other evidence that we remembered.

It's for this reason that I feel compelled to provide the following:

Gift Guide for Forgotten Anniversaries

Forgotten 1st anniversary	Clock (for timing how long you get the silent treatment)
Forgotten 2nd anniversary	China (for eating your slice of humble pie)
Forgotten 3rd anniversary	Crystal (crystal pitcher for bailing out all the hot water you're in)
Forgotten 4th anniversary	Appliances (a refrigerator for storing the ice you'll be getting from the cold shoulder treatment)
Forgotten 5th anniversary	Silverware (to help extract your foot from your mouth after you said, "Thanks for the anniversary card, honey, but it's not our anniversary . . . is it?")

Forgotten 6th anniversary	Wood (for building the dog-house you'll now be living in)
Forgotten 7th anniversary	Desk set (for writing "I will not forget our anniversary" 250 times)
Forgotten 8th anniversary	Linens (for drying those dishes you'll now be doing as an atonement)
Forgotten 12th anniversary	Pearls (as a reminder that you just sank your boat)
Forgotten 25th anniversary	Silver knee pads (for begging forgiveness)
Forgotten 50th anniversary	Gold fillings (to replace the ones that fell out from eating all that crow)

A Date to Communicate

With today's fast-paced schedules, it's easy to forget a special date. But when your spouse does something like this, what it says to you is:

Him:

Her:

If you had to write an anniversary card to your spouse right now, what would it say?

Him:

Her:

> The greatest problem in marriage today is a lack of communication.
>
> Stan Toler
> Author, pastor

50

'Til Debt Do Us Part

Thou wilt keep him in perfect peace, whose mind is stayed on thee: because he trusteth in thee.

Isaiah 26:3

THE subject of money is probably the number one source of stress in a marriage. She charges too much at the mall. He spends too much at the golf course. He wishes she'd let her ATM card cool off once in a while. She wishes he'd quit donating to the Save the Aardvark Society.

A shortage of funds often means short tempers, and if you're not careful, the first of the month can wreak havoc on your relationship.

Who knows how many couples have broken up not because of an affair, not because of a substance abuse problem, but because of bad money management?

In any marriage, there are going to be both plentiful times and lean times. If you don't already know that, you're probably still at your reception. One year you can be on top of the world, paying all your bills on time, enjoying an abundant supply of extra spending money, and the next year you can be standing in an unemployment line, borrowing from your son's coin collection, and having to open that can of mustard greens that's been sitting in the back of your cupboard for four years.

No one's job is 100 percent secure. You have no guarantee that company you work for isn't going to file bankruptcy, or downsize, or simply decide someone else can do your job for a lot less money. No one's health is 100 percent secure either. Who knows if you're going to get sick and not be able to work, or if one of your children will incur unforeseen medical expenses that end up taking most of your income this year?

There aren't any guarantees in life, so your happiness can't be dependent on your situation. It has to come from inside you, and should still be there whether you have all the money in the world or not a single dime.

A Date to Communicate

Do you think you spend too much time arguing over finances?

Him:

Her:

What steps could you take today to give yourself more financial freedom tomorrow?

Him:

Her:

I have learned that only two things are necessary to keep one's wife happy. First let her think she's having her way. And second let her have it.

Lyndon B. Johnson

51
High Finances

I will bless the LORD, who hath given me counsel: my reins also instruct me in the night seasons.

Psalm 16:7

ARGUING over the family finances is nothing new. Couples have been doing it since the beginning of time. Listen in on a conversation that might have taken place between Adam and Eve.

Adam: Eve . . .
Eve: Yes, Adam?
Adam: Where'd you get that?
Eve: Get what?

Adam: That new leaf. I told you we can't afford anything new right now . . . especially since we got kicked out of the garden.

Eve: It's just a leaf, Adam.

Adam: Today it's a leaf, tomorrow it's a whole closet full of them. You didn't charge it, did you?

Eve: No. I know we're over our limit on our Eden Express card.

Adam: So, if you didn't use plastic, what'd you use?

Eve: I've been saving a little each week from the grocery money.

Adam: So that explains the tofu sandwiches.

Eve: I don't understand why you're so upset.

Adam: I'm upset because there wasn't a thing wrong with your old outfit.

Eve: That was last season's leaf. Surely, you don't expect me to be seen in outdated foliage!

Adam: *I'm* still wearing last season's leaf.

Eve: I noticed.

Adam: Look, Eve, is this going to become a habit with you—needing new clothes every time the seasons change?

Eve: I'm a woman. Didn't you read that chapter in the manual?

Adam: Something tells me my disobedience is going to cost me a lot more than I thought!

Eve: You know, I did see this cute little maple leaf jumpsuit . . . and there was this birch swimsuit that was absolutely adorable. I even saw a pinstriped elm leaf for you.

Adam: You know we can't afford all th . . . pinstriped, huh?

Eve: It was the only one left. They close in twenty minutes. We could make it if we hurry.

Adam: Oh, all right, let's go. But thousands of years from now, every time a man has to go shopping with his wife, he's gonna blame all this on me!

A Date to Communicate

How much of your time and energy is spent worrying about finances?

Him:

Her:

Financial experts tell us that the way out of debt is to spend less than we make. Simple as that. What positive steps do you feel you could start taking today to cut down your expenses?

Him:

Her:

> Any married man should forget his past mistakes. There's no use in two people remembering the same thing.
>
> Source unknown

52
No Puzzle

For thou art my rock and my fortress;
therefore for thy name's sake lead me, and
guide me.

Psalm 31:3

A friend of mine, Katie Brooks Lee, is constructing a rock wall on her property. It's a mortarless wall—they're popular in the Nashville, Tennessee, area. The rocks, or slate, are laid one on top of each other, fitting together like a giant puzzle. A rock that has an indentation on its right side is fitted perfectly with another rock that has a protrusion on the same side. This matching up of shapes and sizes requires some time and effort, but the payoff is well worth it. Anyone who has seen these walls are captivated by their beauty and intrigued by their simplistic engineering.

If we think of our married lives as a rock wall, with each rock representing one day, we'll find that some of those days may have had a jagged edge here or some erosion there, while others were smooth and level. To build the wall of our lives, though, each one of those rocks is needed. We need the smooth ones to stack on top of other smooth ones, but we also need those rocks with a few chips and indentations to balance out the areas where we may have been protruding a little too much out of proportion.

Then, when all is said and done, we can look back and see how the events of our lives—the good times, the bad times, the fun times, and the not so fun times—have all fit together. We'll be able to clearly see how each incident has helped maintain balance in our lives and made our wall a sturdy fortress. It won't be puzzling then.

A Date to Communicate

Are you having a difficult time seeing how the rocks of your life are fitting together?

Him:

Her:

Why do you think it's important to stand back and look at the whole of our lives instead of each individual day?

Him:

Her:

It was important for me that my wife is strong because I could have become very controlling. Her strength has made our marriage stronger. She's neither a servant nor a clone, but my partner and friend.

Merritt McKay
Vice president,
Nazarene Publishing Company

53
Trading Places

The sleep of a labouring man is sweet,
whether he eat little or eat much.

Ecclesiastes 5:12

MY husband doesn't spend a lot of time in the kitchen. I don't blame him. I've been responsible for more than my share of kitchen disasters, so I guess the room brings back too many bad memories. But every once in a while, out of the clear blue, he'll volunteer to cook dinner. This is always an experience because my husband likes to get creative with food. He once made a meatloaf in the shape of Israel for a youth pastor who had just returned home from the Holy Land. It was pretty good, although Tel Aviv looked a little crispy.

Another time, he made a pot of chili for a deacon and his family. It was so salty even Lot's wife would have complained.

He's had barbecues that were mistaken for brush fires, scrambled eggs with enough shell to break your bridgework, and soufflés that never did rise to the occasion.

Still, it's kind of nice when he gives me a break from the kitchen. The family likes it, too. And I'm sure he appreciates it whenever I take over one of his regular chores for a change.

This week, why not give your spouse a break and do something that's normally not your job to do? Who knows, husbands, you just might discover you're a gourmet chef. Or maybe you'll realize that laundry was your missed calling. And wives, you might find out that you have a knack for plumbing, electrical repairs, or putting in that room addition you've always wanted.

After switching jobs for a day or so, you might decide your own chores don't look so bad after all. One thing's for sure, though: you'll never know until you give it a try.

A Date to Communicate

What chore of yours would you love for your spouse to try doing for a while?

Him:

Her:

What chore of your spouse's would you like to give a try?

Him:

Her:

I feel the secret to a good marriage is a good friendship. It's also important to have the same vision, the same heart, the same direction for your lives.

Marty Christesson
Missionary, comedian,
comedy writer

54
Of Timely Concern

Be kindly affectioned one to another with brotherly love; in honour preferring one another.

Romans 12:10

ALTHOUGH there have been studies telling us what percentage of our lives is spent sleeping, eating, watching television, going to church, going to school, driving, and talking on the telephone, I've often wondered if anyone has ever determined how much of our life is spent waiting for our spouse to get ready.

Women usually get blamed for being the slow dresser, but sometimes it's the man who makes the family late. Regardless, before a couple exchanges those vows, a fast dresser should know what he or she is getting into by being "unequally yoked" with a slow dresser. By marrying outside your dressing speed, you're doomed to get most of your daily exercise pacing, looking at your watch, and saying profound things like, "Let's go!"

If you don't mind a life like this, then by all means, go ahead and say, "I do." If, however, you want to see more of that play than the curtain call or hear more of the sermon than "and now in closing," you'll do well to have a healthy discussion about the problem *before* the wedding.

By the same token, irrational, compulsive clock watchers can be just as irritating as the slow dresser. People who threaten to jump off the ledge of Big Ben if they're one minute late probably have other underlying compulsive behaviors you might want to steer away from, too.

The answer, of course, is a happy medium. It's important to do our best to be on time. If, however, due to some unforeseen circumstances, we're still going to be late, it's not worth having the fight of our lives over it. How we treat our spouse in *all* situations is far more important than punctuality. We should be more concerned with the impression we make on the person we live with than the impression we make on others.

A Date to Communicate

If you're a perpetual latecomer, but promptness is important to your spouse, what can you do to help change your habits?

Him:

Her:

If, in your compulsion to be prompt, you tend to say hurtful things to your spouse, what steps can you take to change?

Him:

Her:

The secret to a happy marriage is to quit looking for happiness for yourself and spend your time looking for ways to make your spouse happy. Whatever you sow, that's what you reap!

Kathi Mills
Author, editor, Bible teacher
Married seventeen years

55
Overnight Change

Put on the new man, which after God is
created in righteousness and true holiness.

Ephesians 4:24

WOULDN'T it be great if the next time you
need a new roof on your house, all you have to
do is make one telephone call and that very night
a crew shows up at your home, fixes your roof
while you sleep (their hammering doesn't even
disturb you), and the next morning there wouldn't
be the slightest hint that a work crew had even

216

been there. All their nails would be picked up, there wouldn't be any tread marks left by their trucks, and no empty soda cans would be lining your driveway. You'd have a brand-new roof without having to be inconvenienced in any way. One call, simple as that, and all your problems are over. That'd be terrific, wouldn't it?

But repairs aren't that easy. A crew will usually show up while you're wide awake or at six in the morning when you least want them there. You'll have to deal with the dust, nails, and trash littering your driveway. And then, of course, there's the noise. Ah, yes, the noise. But there's no way around it. If you want the repairs done, and done right, there's a certain amount of inconvenience you're going to have to put up with.

It's the same when we desire changes in our spouse. They're not going to happen overnight while we sleep. And they're not going to come without some adjustments on our part. No matter how much we want to wake up and have that person lying next to us be a completely different individual than when we closed our eyes the night before, it's not going to happen. Change isn't that easy. Behaviors aren't learned overnight and they can't be unlearned overnight either. In fact, some behaviors are so much a part of who the individual has become that only God can change them.

But if you're a wife waiting for your husband's behavior to change, or if you're a husband waiting for your wife's behavior to change, there is something you can do in the meantime. Instead of focusing on the construction site, wondering when in the world the repairs are ever going to be made, focus instead on how beautiful that new "roof" is going to look once the work is completed.

A Date to Communicate

What changes would you like to see take place in your spouse?

Him:

Her:

What changes would your spouse like to see take place in you?

Him:

Her:

> If our spouses don't treat us as they should, we ought to be very grateful.

Anonymous

56
No Words Needed

And this I pray, that your love may abound yet more and more in knowledge and in all judgment.

Philippians 1:9

It's been said that couples who have been married for years eventually end up looking like one another. In some instances that does seem to be the case. But that's not the only way to tell if a couple has been married a long time.

You Know You've Been Married a Long Time When . . .

—you can carry on an entire conversation from across a crowded room using only your eyes.

—you haven't finished one of your own sentences in years.

—now when you hold the door open for your wife, it's so she won't hit it while carrying in the piano.

—you're not sure whether her backseat driving's gotten better or your hearing aid's just not picking her voice up.

—your spouse accidentally kicks you under the dinner table and you know it's no accident.

—these days candlelight dinners mean a blackout, not a love-in.

A Date to Communicate

What steps can you take today to keep the honeymoon alive in your marriage?

Him:

Her:

What positive things come from a long married life?

Him:

Her:

> Marriage is like a rare coin—sometimes it's heads and sometimes it's tails, but it's always of great value and worth. It's something to be treasured.
>
> Kathy Cadle
> Homemaker

57
Visibility Zero

Thou shalt guide me with thy counsel, and afterward receive me to glory.

Psalm 73:24

ONE night as my husband and I were driving home from the Knoxville area, we got caught in a downpour. We couldn't see the cars next to us, the cars in front of us, or the truck behind us (although we had no trouble hearing his brakes). Visibility was near zero. It was like being stuck in a car wash without the giant brushes. We would have pulled over to the side of the road and waited for the weather to clear up, but who knew where the side of the road was? All we could do was keep going, looking straight ahead, and hoping and praying we'd drive out of it eventually.

After fifteen or twenty minutes of white-knuckling it along Interstate 40, we did come out of it, and for the entire remainder of the trip to Nashville, the road was dry, the sky was clear, and everyone was back up to speed again.

Sometimes life feels like you're caught in a downpour and you'll never be able to drive out of it. You can't see the road in front of you. You can't see the road behind you. And you feel like you're about to be run over by a twelve-wheeler at any moment. Maybe there are those around you who could offer help should you become stranded, but you don't know it because your problem has you so blinded that visibility is zero. You feel like pulling over to the side of the road and giving up, but you can't even see the side of the road. That's when you've got to keep going, keeping your eyes focused on your destination and trusting that the downpour won't last forever. It won't either. No matter how bad things look at the time, eventually you're going to drive out of it. Your sky will be clear again, and you'll know undeniably that God's promise of a rainbow was not only for the world, but for our lives as well.

A Date to Communicate

Are you in the middle of a downpour right now? Talk about it.

Why do you think it's important to never lose sight of the fact that our problems won't last forever, but God's love and providence will?

Him:

Her:

> So live that you wouldn't be ashamed to sell the family parrot to the town gossip.
>
> Will Rogers

58
Fit for Marriage

The way of a slothful man is as a hedge of thorns.

Proverbs 15:19

MY husband is an avid jogger. He runs several miles every day, and I'm right there with him. Of course, he usually waves me on because the exhaust fumes from the car are choking him.

If you haven't caught on by now, I'm not into exercise. The only time I break into a sweat is when I've got a fever. It's important, though, for marriage partners to pay attention to their physical well being. Our spouses love us and want us to stick around for that twenty-fifth, fiftieth, or even seventy-fifth anniversary. They worry when we ladle country gravy over our cheese and bacon omelet or have that fourth brownie. They're afraid that we're going to pay a price for our sedentary lifestyle, a price they're not ready for us to pay.

Sometimes their concern can get irritating, though.

We have a friend whose husband is constantly reminding her of the things she shouldn't eat. While ordering the enchilada plate—"That's going to keep you up all night." As she snacks on a potato chip—"Do you have any idea what the fat content of one of those is?" The second she takes a lick from an icecream cone—"Your cholesterol level's going to go through the roof!" Whatever she eats, he has something to say about it. Who wants that kind of micro management? It's like eating a box of chocolates while standing on a bathroom scale. What fun is that?

Compromise is the answer here. Micro managers need to let their spouses make a few decisions, and the recipients of the surveillance need to show some responsibility for their own well being. Then, when it's time to celebrate that golden anniversary, they'll both be around to show up.

A Date to Communicate

Do you honestly think you take good care of yourself?

Him:

Her:

List some reasons why you think it's important to pay attention to your health.

Him:

Her:

Unconditional love eventually
brings out the best in the recipient.

Anonymous

59

Sabotaged

Whoso keepeth his mouth and his tongue keepeth his soul from troubles.

Proverbs 21:23

I knew a lady once who would never allow anyone to say anything bad about her husband. She was very vocal about this and announced it regularly, as if taking some sort of noble stand. The only problem was, she was the only one saying bad things about her husband, and she'd say them every chance she got.

Mixed messages. Husbands and wives can't have it both ways. If a wife verbally tears down her husband, or a husband verbally tears down his wife, they can't expect others to respect them.

If you truly love someone, you're going to want to present them in the best light to those around you. Their reputation should be as important as your own. If you list all their shortcomings in your monthly newsletter to friends, it'll be hard to sound sincere when you're bragging about them in your Christmas letter.

A Date to Communicate

When you talk about your spouse to others, are you more positive or negative?

Him:

Her:

How would you feel if you heard that your spouse had said something derogatory about you?

Him:

Her:

Always trust each other. Don't go to bed mad. Try to work it out.

Thedy Ann Edwards
Married seventy years

60

I Do . . . for Today, at Least

But if ye forgive not men their trespasses, neither will your Father forgive your
trespasses.

Matthew 6:15

THE old television show "Divorce Court" once
aired an episode featuring a man who was
divorcing his wife because she served weenies
and beans to his boss for dinner. Her husband
had hardly given her any warning that company
was coming. At least, that was her defense. She
said she didn't have time to run to the store, so

she served the only thing she had in the house—weenies and beans.

I don't recall whether they were granted the divorce. I doubt it. Back then, it was a lot more difficult to dissolve a marriage. Today, the divorce might have been granted before the first station break.

No one ever said that marriage would be easy. Any time you put two human beings, often two totally *opposite* human beings, in the same living space, there's bound to be a few conflicts. Conflicts don't mean the marriage is doomed, however. Sometimes it's those very conflicts that help make a marriage stronger.

As a society, though, we've made it too easy to get out of marriage at the first sign of trouble. Instead of working out our problems, we head for the door, and by doing so, we're cheating ourselves out of one of the best parts of marriage—the fun of making up.

My husband's parents divorced when he was twelve years old. He remembers the endless arguing and admits things got a lot more peaceful after the divorce. What he remembers even more, though, are the many things he missed out on by not having a father around.

233

No matter how amicable a divorce is, the severance of a marriage leaves behind a significant amount of damage—some of it is repairable, much of it is irreparable. And all too often, it's the children who suffer most.

When we stand before a minister or justice of the peace and repeat those sacred vows, divorce is the last thing on our minds. Perhaps more marriages would survive if it remained the last thing on couples' minds throughout the marriage, too.

A Date to Communicate

What do the vows you spoke at your wedding mean to you personally?

Him:

Her:

What do you think it means to be loved and to love unconditionally?

Him:

Her:

> Marriage is like a poker game. If you get dealt a good hand, you keep it!
>
> Mike Kowalski
> Drummer for the Beach Boys

Marriage Coupons

"GET OUT OF SHOPPING" FREE CARD

The undersigned is hereby relieved of any obligation to accompany his wife shopping. This card is good for the period of one day only, following which all shopping duties will resume.

Name:_____

Date:_____

"FREE DESSERT"

This card entitles bearer to one dessert with no mention of the calories included therein.

"HONEY, DO" FREE PASS

Bearer is entitled to one free pass on any item on his "Honey, Do" list.

(NOTE: This pass may not be reproduced in order to obtain multiple copies. Offenders will be prosecuted to the fullest extent of the law.)

COUPON FOR ONE KISS

Present this coupon during any disagreement. Kiss must be given immediately.

KITCHEN RELIEF

This card entitles bearer freedom from one night's worth of dirty dishes, cooking, sweeping, or mopping. Spouse will take bearer of card to restaurant of choice.

OFFICIAL DRIVE ALONE CARD

Since there may only be one operator of a moving vehicle at a time, it is hereby declared that I, the person behind the wheel, shall be the official driver. Advice from the passenger side may be heeded or ignored at the sole discretion of said driver.

_____
(signature)

ONE "MISSING CHECK" PASS

Bearer of this card is entitled to one missing check number in the check register. If, after one week, bearer still doesn't have a clue who the check was written to, account may then be canceled.

On this date _____, the undersigned is hereby authorized to throw away any undergarment found on the floor.

_____
(signature)

OFFENSE EXPIRATION DATE

The following offenses will now have an expiration date. Prior to this date, these offenses have not been bound by any time limits. However, in the ongoing pursuit of peace on earth, an expiration date will now be added. Once the expiration date has expired, the infraction cannot be brought up, no matter how applicable it seems at the time.

OFFENSE (His) _____

EXPIRATION DATE _____

(Offense Expiration Date Card Continued)

OFFENSE (Hers) _____

EXPIRATION DATE _____

_____

_____

_____

_____

The bearer of this card is entitled to one uninterrupted nap.

_____

MALE PAIN VERIFICATION FORM
Patient:

Symptoms:

This is to verify that the above named patient is indeed suffering from the aforementioned symptoms. Contrary to what his loved ones may believe, this is truly the worst case of _____ (insert problem: head cold, hang nail, etc.) known to man. If ICU unit is not available, please render care at home.

This card entitles bearer to one guilt-free game of golf.

_____

Getting to Know You

Tell about the moment when you first realized your mate was the one for you:

Him: _____

_____

Her: _____

_____

What qualities were you looking for in a marriage partner?

His answer: _____

_____

Her answer: _____

_____

You're most proud of your mate because:

His answer: _____

_____

Her answer: _____

_____

What is your definition of a happy marriage?

His answer: _____

_____

Her answer: _____

_____

If you could improve one thing about your marriage, what would it be?

His answer: _____

_____

Her answer: _____

_____

Other than hearing the words "I love you," what is your favorite way to be shown love?

His answer: _____

_____

Her answer: _____

_____

What do you respect most about your mate?

His answer: _____

_____

Her answer: _____

_____

What do you feel is your mate's best physical feature?

His answer: _____

Her answer: _____

What do you like most about your mate's personality?

His answer: _____

_____

Her answer: _____

_____

What first attracted you to your mate?

His answer: _____

_____

Her answer: _____

_____

What song best describes your relationship?

His answer: _____

_____

Her answer: _____

_____

List three things you'd like to accomplish in life:

His answer:

1. _____

2. _____

3. _____

Her answer:

1. _____

2. _____

3. _____

What melts your heart?

Him: _____

_____

Her: _____

_____

What area of your own life do you wish you could improve?

Him: _____

_____

Her: _____

_____

What I cherish most about our marriage is:

Him: _____

_____

Her: _____

_____

If I could tell my spouse one thing, it would be:

Him: _____

_____

Her: _____

_____

Is there something between the two of you that you're having a difficult time forgiving?

Him: _____

_____

Her: _____

_____

Knowing how unhealthy it is for both you and your relationship, why do you think you're continuing to harbor that hurt?

Him: _____

_____

Her: _____

_____

The funniest thing my spouse ever did was:

Him: _____

_____

Her: _____

_____

If I had to write down the recipe for a lasting marriage, the five most important ingredients would be:

Him:

1. _____

2. _____

3. _____

4. _____

5. _____

Her:

1. _____

2. _____

3. _____

4. _____

5. _____

What pets did you have growing up?

Him: _____

_____

Her: _____

_____

Why were they special to you?

Him: _____

_____

Her: _____

_____

What's your favorite color?

Him: _____

_____

Her: _____

_____

If you had your life to live over again, what one event would you change?

Him: _____

_____

_____

Her: _____

_____

_____

What is the one place you've always wanted to go someday?

Him: _____

Her: _____

List three times during your marriage when you were wrong about something. (No blank lines allowed.)

Him:

1. _____

250

2. _____

3. _____

Her:

1. _____

2. _____

3. _____

If they ever make a movie about the two of you, who would you want to play you?

Him: _____

Her: _____

What words of wisdom would you say to a couple who are about to take their marriage vows?

Him: _____

_____

Her: _____

_____

Martha Bolton has been a staff writer for comedian Bob Hope for over fifteen years. She has written more than thirty books, and her *Cafeteria Lady* column in the Focus on the Family teen girls' magazine, *Brio,* has been a favorite with readers since it began. She and her husband, Russ, divide their time between Nashville, Tennessee, and Los Angeles, California.

If Mr. Clean Calls, Tell Him I'm Not In!

**A Look at Family Life
by Bob Hope's comedy writer**

TAKING A TONGUE-IN-CHEEK look at pressures that affect every family, like oversleeping, burning dinner, and warding off pesky telephone solicitors, Bolton enables readers to gain the perspective that God is there and cares even when it's "one of those days."

"Martha Bolton finds the fun in the familiar, the mirth in the mundane, the belly laughs in the bellyaches of everyday living. She can turn a chore into a chuckle, and a problem into a punchline. Laughter is not reserved for the stage, screen, and television; it should be a part of everyday life—from breakfast through to the bedtime snack. So enjoy this book of Martha Bolton's, but remember one thing: She's my writer."

—**Bob Hope**

ISBN 0-8007-5729-7   144 pages $4.99

Don't Wake Me 'til after Lunch!

WITH A GOOD SENSE for the wild and wacky, Martha Bolton offers today's teenagers a collection of forty-three fun commentaries on life, including "Confessions of a Phoneaholic" and "It's Time to Clean Your Bedroom When . . ." Her hilarious capers and outrageous stunts give readers a welcome chance to find their funny sides amid the awkwardness of adolescence. Teens may find they can't stifle their laughter— no matter how hard they try!

ISBN 0-8007-5730-0   160 pages $4.99